The Bathtub Reader

AN AMUSING MISCELLANY FOR
THE DISCERNING MADEMOISELLE

Carrie Bell and Amy Helmes

CIDER MILL
PRESS

BOOK
PUBLISHERS

Kennebunkport, Maine

13-Digit ISBN: 978-1-60433-010-6
10-Digit ISBN: 1-60433-01102

This book may be ordered by mail from the publisher.
Please include $2.00 for postage and handling.
Please support your local bookseller first!

Books published by Cider Mill Press Book Publishers are available at special discounts for bulk purchases in the United States by corporations, institutions, and other organizations. For more information, please contact the publisher.

Cider Mill Press Book Publishers
"Where good books are ready for press"
12 Port Farm Road
Kennebunkport, Maine 04046

Visit us on the Web!
www.cidermillpress.com

Design by Alicia Freile
Typography: Arabesque Ornaments, Bulmer MT, Dorchester Script MT, and Futura
Printed in China

2 3 4 5 6 7 8 9 0

Contents

Soak It All In

Picture a spacious porcelain clawed foot tub brimming with bubbles atop water just this side of steaming. At the far end of the bath peek your ten toes painted a vibrant, diva-worthy red. The faucet drops a slow and steady, meditative drip, and for the moment, all is right in your calm little corner of the world. Miraculously, you've got no immediate obligations and the better part of an hour before your fingertips start heading in the direction of Pruneville. But what you really need to make this luxurious soak complete is a good book. Something not too taxing, something that will amuse, astonish…something that will leave you a little more enlightened when you emerge from this soothing sanctuary and return to life's everyday chaos.

Enter *The Bathtub Reader*, your complete powder room primer, full of fun factoids, astonishing anecdotes, and miscellaneous musings certain to delight the most inquiring female mind. Journey back into history to discover ancient beauty rituals, centuries-old courtship customs and the stories behind your favorite fashion finds. Learn about the women who left their own unique stamp on the world, and glean little-known facts about today's hottest celebs. You can even devour a whole chapter on food without gaining an ounce!

Consider *The Bathtub Reader* your ultimate ode *de toilet*. After all, if you're going to be accused of hogging the bathroom for hours on end to carry out your painstaking primping procedures, you may as well keep some curiously compelling reading material on hand to pass the time. When you finally emerge looking pretty as a picture, you'll be equally polished in the realm of pop culture and general knowledge. Men have been sneaking off to the bathroom to read for ages, and we don't think that they should have all the fun. So go ahead, sit back, and soak it all in…just don't drop this book in the suds. While *The Bathtub Reader* may be a lot of things, one thing that it's *not* is waterproof.

CHAPTER 1

Beauty Secrets

NATURAL BEAUTY? Perhaps it exists in some fantasy realm where your skinny jeans always fit and broccoli tastes like cupcakes. But for the rest of us hapless souls prone to waking up most mornings bearing a marked resemblance to the Bride of Frankenstein, we know better. Putting our best face forward is neither easy nor breezy. Rather, it entails marathon sessions of plucking, spraying, dying, painting, and curling, not to mention more buffing and waxing than a drive-thru car wash. Women go to great lengths to look good—some even relying on flesh-eating marine life—and this chapter barely scratches the surface of our girly-girl obsessions with beauty. As for anyone who says, "It's what's on the inside that counts," well, tell that to the trillion-dollar cosmetics industry. They may beg to differ.

LIP SERVICE

A crimson pout has long been the glam girl's secret weapon for achieving instant sex appeal. Here's a mouthful of interesting lipstick lore.

The first lipstick, estimated to be more than five thousand years old, was found in the Sumerian region of Ur. Lip color was also prevalent among ancient Egyptians, Syrians, Babylonians, Persians, and Greeks. The trend fell on hard times in the Middle Ages (when a made-up woman was believed to be an incarnation of Satan) and the 19th century (when only "loose women" and actresses painted their faces).

Until the government began regulating its production in 1938, lipstick could deliver the kiss of death, literally. Many contained toxic substances like arsenic, lead, and mercury. Post World War II, it was common practice to use crushed insect bodies in the pigment. In 1924, the New York Board of Health considered banning lipstick out of fear that men would be poisoned by kissing lipstick-laden lips. As recently as the 1960s, some cosmetic companies were still using harmful red dyes.

Lipstick wasn't always a woman thing. Early Egyptians of both sexes preferred a blue-black shade and went to their graves with rouge pots for afterlife touch-ups. Certain lip colors indicated social standing and rank among men in ancient Rome, and during the Baroque era (1660–1789), respectable men of the British and French aristocracy dabbled in lip painting, aiming for a round, pearl-like pout.

Application methods have changed a lot over the years as well. Fingers have always been an option. Egyptians used a wet wood stick. A popular product in the 1700s was Spanish Rouge, which was basically a pad of hair similar to a dish-scrubbing pad filled with red coloring instead of soap. Stage actresses of the 1840s brushed on color with a rabbit's foot while late 19th century folks used bits of silk or cotton gauze twisted into a plug filled with color.

Before Maurice Levy designed the first modern sticks in sliding metal tubes in 1915, the pigment came in pots and was called lip rouge. Today, there are three variations of the bullet-shaped stick: the fishtail (angled on both sides), the teardrop (a pointed tip angled on one side), and the wedge (a more rounded tip angled on one side).

England's Queen Elizabeth I was such a huge proponent of makeup that during her reign it was sometimes used as currency. The youth-obsessed queen allegedly had close to half an inch of pigment on her lips when she died.

Recruiting Tinseltown talent like Halle Berry, Julianne Moore, and Queen Latifah to hawk lipstick is not a modern phenomenon. Earlier screen sirens, including Jean Harlow, Clara Bow, Ella Raines, and Elizabeth Taylor all worked for Max Factor between 1930 and 1960.

In 1952, Revlon's Fire and Ice campaign caused quite a stir, making Fire and Ice the company's most popular lip color. The then-scandalous ad featured model Dorian Leigh in a silver sequined dress and scarlet wrap asking, "Are you made for Fire and Ice?" To find out, women were challenged to answer a series of fifteen oh-so-daring questions, including, "Have you ever danced with your shoes off?" or "Would you streak you hair platinum without consulting your husband?"

In 2000, Hard Candy introduced a line of lipstick laced with caffeine and menthol that promised to deliver the same rush as a double espresso. The zing was absorbed through the skin upon application. The initial three shades were Lipachino, Latte Lip, and Café O Lip.

HAIR APPARENT

*Most girls would do just about anything for a quality coif,
but many probably aren't aware of this hair-raising history. Here's your chance to brush up.*

Camel-hair brushes are not actually
made from the pelts of those desert
dromedaries. Instead, they are typically
made from the hair of squirrels, ponies,
goats, sheep, oxen, or bears.

Anthropologists believe that the earliest humans used sticks, stones, thorns, and bones as hair adornments. An ornate type of hairpin called a bodkin was fashionable during the Renaissance. Bobby pins were first introduced to America in 1916 and earned their name because many women used the pins to keep their hip new bob haircuts in place. (In England, incidentally, they're called "Kirby grips" after one of the original manufacturers of the product in the United Kingdom.)

During the 1960s, some women achieved the voluminous bouffant look by sleeping with their hair wrapped around cylindrical orange juice cans. Conversely, those hoping for sleek, straight hair would iron their tresses with a genuine clothes iron.

Even the women of ancient Rome lived by the credo that blondes have more fun. They showed off by donning wigs supplied from the heads and faces of the fair-haired barbarians that their husbands conquered on battlefields.

In the 1940s, scores of women copied the glamorous mane of actress Veronica Lake. But during WWII, when too many female factory workers got their tresses tangled up in the machinery, the U.S. government appealed to Lake, who participated in publicity campaigns cautioning ladies about the hazards of long locks.

As the originators of "mall hair," female aristocrats in 18th century France opted for elaborate, extreme feats of engineering held together with lard and grease. They incorporated birdcages holding live butterflies, cascading waterfalls, or models of sailing vessels depicting naval battles. The 'dos were so tall that women often resorted to kneeling in carriages or riding with their heads stuck out the window. The weight of these hairstyles caused back problems. The complicated coifs also attracted vermin, thus inspiring the phrase "rat's nest."

A person typically loses seventy-five to one-hundred scalp hairs every day, while thirty-five meters of hair fiber is produced on the average adult head over that same time period.

Researchers at the University of Edinburgh in Scotland determined that women with red hair have a higher threshold for pain than blondes or brunettes. Maybe that's a good thing, too, seeing as how some people believe redheads are more prone to beestings!

In the early part of the 20th century, women who dyed their hair were considered to be promiscuous or morally suspect. Wanting to eliminate the stigma of their product, Clairol devised an ad campaign that asked, "Does she or doesn't she? Only her hairdresser knows for sure!"

THE RAZOR'S EDGE

Women have sought to be smooth operators for centuries. Here's a look at the lengths we'll go to (and the nicks that we'll suffer) en route to our beauty ideal.

In ancient Greece, women removed hair from their legs by singeing it off with a lamp. One famous male shaver was Alexander the Great. He refused to enter into battle sporting so much as a five o'clock shadow, thereby starting the trend for men to go beardless.

The Roman emperor Nero's wife used depilatory creams to remove unwanted body hair. At the time, such creams included ingredients such as she-goat gall, bat blood, and powdered viper.

Those "plucky" ladies of medieval Europe adopted the practice of removing all hair from their eyebrows, eyelashes, and foreheads to accommodate the era's fashionable headdresses. Queen Elizabeth I was among those adopting the bald-faced look.

In Russia, Peter the Great is said to have detested beards so much that he taxed any man who grew one.

Today, North American women are more likely to shave their body hair than women in any other region of the world. This may be due to an ad in a 1915 edition of *Harper's Bazaar* magazine that featured a model in a sleeveless evening gown showing, for the first time in fashion history, bare armpits. The ad stated: "Summer dress and modern dancing combine to make necessary the removal of objectionable hair."

In the early 20th century, the Wilkinson Sword Company, which produced razor blades for men, designed a marketing campaign to convince American women that underarm hair was both unhygienic and unfeminine. Women wholeheartedly bought into the company's message as razor blade sales doubled in two years.

When WWII caused shortages of metal, 1940s femmes turned to the most readily available razor blade alternative: course sandpaper (which surely rubbed them the wrong way!)

Entertainment Tonight host Mary Hart was so dependent on her sexy legs as a mainstay of her career that she had them ensured by Lloyd's of London for one million dollars. But she wasn't the first to have done so. Betty Grable, Jamie Lee Curtis, Marlene Dietrich, and Tina Turner have all taken out insurance on their gams. (Men on that roster: Fred Astaire, Michael Flatley, and David Beckham.)

Schick Quattro for Women coined made-up lingo on the company's Web site to describe certain shaving phenomena, including "Bathtub Tinsel" (little pieces of shaved hair and soap left in the tub after the water drains) and "Chastity Pelt" (intentionally not shaving prior to a date as a way of ensuring you'll behave).

Manicur-ious

Whether blood-red daggers are your thing or pretty in pink is more to your liking, keep these nail facts on file—and at your fingertips.

In ancient China, circa 3000 B.C., nail color was a symbol of social status. Royal digits in the Ming Dynasty would have been brushed in black and red.

When women stopped wearing dress gloves in the 1900s, polished nails made a dramatic comeback. Most ladies opted for transparent polish to add natural-looking luster or subtle rose tints to signify good health. At this point in time, polish came in powder form.

Madame Mille, a famous French manicurist, was among the first people to use liquid polish on clients. Shades of deep crimson were trendy in the 1930s although Parisians briefly toyed with emerald green nails.

The Q-Tip, a common manicure implement, was originally sold under the name Baby Gays. In 1926, the name expanded to Q-Tips Baby Gays. Eventually, the whole "gay baby" thing was dropped altogether. The "Q" stands for quality, and "Tips" refers to the product's cotton ends.

Half the battle of marketing polish is coming up with an eye-catching name for the hundreds of shades available. OPI has become famous for their unique and imaginative names. Here's a sampling of their most inventive ones: Don't Socra-Tease Me, I'm Not Really a Waitress, Lincoln Park After Dark, Did Someone Say PARTY!, Aphrodite's Pink Nightie, Fiji Weegee Fawn, Melon of Troy, Pistol Packin' Pink, Who Comes Up With These Names? (Yep, it's a shade).

Vaseline petroleum jelly is great for keeping cuticles moisturized, but its creator, a Brooklyn chemist named Robert Chesebrough, also swore by eating the goop! After realizing that the same pasty residue that clogged oil workers' drills was effective at soothing burns and cuts, he began marketing the miracle product and reportedly ate a spoonful daily. Vaseline's uses are myriad, from soothing chapped lips and taming unruly eyebrows to removing makeup and unsticking gum caught in hair. It's good for just about anything, except, well, on bread with peanut butter.

Nails grow more quickly in summer than in winter. Men's nails grow more quickly than women's.

While French manicures may have originated in the 18th century, ORLY International claims to have created the modern version in the mid-1970s. Founder Jeff Pink noticed the look on Parisian runway models who used white pencil to lighten nail tips. When a Hollywood producer asked Pink to develop a neutral nail color flexible enough to match multiple wardrobe changes, he remembered those models and duplicated the idea.

EXTREME MAKEOVER

Bold and beautiful or weird and wacky? Let's be honest. It probably depends on if it works.

A London salon called Hari's offers a facial made from nightingale droppings. It's a method thought up by Japanese geishas, who used droppings in facemasks and to remove their heavy makeup. The same salon also features a hair treatment utilizing bull semen, which is advertised as "Viagra for hair."

Actress Catherine Zeta-Jones has been known to keep her brunette mane full of bounce and body by sudsing up—with beer, that is. It's a tip she learned from her grandmother, but she confesses that one unfortunate after-effect is smelling like a frat house. In other malt-beverage beauty news, family-owned Czech brewery Chodovar offers customers an opportunity to relax in skin-rejuvenating "beer baths."

Preparation H hemorrhoid cream is a staple of many hopeful beauty queens, some of whom use the medicinal ointment to remove under-eye puffiness!

You've heard about BOTOX injections on the face, but what about in the armpits? Before walking the red carpet, some starlets shoot toxin into their underarms to paralyze sweat glands, ensuring that they won't leave pit stains on their borrowed designer frocks.

A salon in Beverly Hills, California, offers facials made with 24K gold, while "crushed pearl" facials are also popular among spa patrons with too much moolah.

Why expend energy buffing your feet when you can find Nemo to do it for you? It's trendy in Tokyo to soak your barking dogs in shallow tubs filled with small fish that nibble away at dead skin, leaving the sole surface silky smooth.

Just call it "modern mummification." An L.A. salon called Suddenly Slimmer promises that, after their hour-long mineral body-wrap treatment, clients can lose six to twenty inches of fat. They also offer a face-taping technique to help restore elasticity to sagging skin.

Swiss skin care line La Prairie offers a "Caviar Collection" featuring—you guessed it—fish eggs. Researchers say roe is loaded with protein, vitamins, and minerals, and helps speed the natural production of collagen.

BY THE NUMBERS

1

Out of every 12 women, the number who say they've felt guilty enough about leaving lipstick smudges on clothes that they tried on at a store that they ended up purchasing said stained item

3

Number of months the effects of a single BOTOX treatment last

4 to 9

Pounds of lipstick the average woman consumes in her lifetime

8

The century, B.C. in which an
Indian physician, Sushruta,
is said to have performed
the first rhinoplasty

9

Number of original saleswomen selling
cosmetics for Mary Kay in 1963;
the sales force exceeded 1.6 million
by 2005

31

*Percent of American teenage girls
who are overweight (15 percent are
categorized as obese)*

36-18-33

What Barbie's measurements would be if she were a real person (According to a study done by the University Central Hospital in Helsinki, Finland, she would lack the required 17 percent body fat necessary for menstruation.)

40

Tom Cruise's age when he got braces to correct his misaligned bite

50

Percent of people who join a gym who will become erratic users or dropouts within a couple of months

50

Percent of adult women who experience adult acne

92 *Percent of women who wear lipstick regularly*

$800

Cost of a haircut performed by Madonna and Gwyneth Paltrow's stylist, Orlando Pita, of New York's Orlo salon

$1,000

*Average cost per tooth for veneers
through U.S. dentists*

1973

The year that the term
cellulite was coined to describe
those dastardly dimples

$2,100

Cost of a three-week supply of Crème de la Mer's Essence, the world's most expensive face cream, which was introduced in 2005 and features seaweed as a primary ingredient

$8,000

Amount one of Cher's wigs was valued at when it was stolen in 2003

8,660,000

Number of Web results you would get if you Googled "wrinkles"

11.5 million

Total number of cosmetic procedures (surgical and non-surgical) performed in the United States in 2006 (403,684 of those were liposuction)

114 million

Number of visits consumers make to massage/bodywork therapists annually

$12.4 BILLION

Amount Americans spent on cosmetic procedures in 2005 according to the American Society for Aesthetic Plastic Surgery

I'm tired of all this nonsense about
beauty being only skin-deep.
That's deep enough. What do you want,

an adorable pancreas?

—Jean Kerr

Sex appeal is fifty percent **what
you've got** and fifty percent
what people **think** you've got.

—Sophia Loren

Kiss and make up—

but too much make-up

has ruined many a kiss.

—Mae West

Lipstick is to the face
what punctuation is
to a sentence.

Get enough sleep and enough sex.
If you don't get enough of either
it will end up showing on your face.

—Kim Hume

I'll make some concessions
if the request is reasonable.
If someone tells me to comb my hair,
I'll comb my hair.
If someone tells me to dye it blond,
they can go to hell.

—Jane Wallace

Nature gives you the face you have when you are twenty. Life shapes the face you have at thirty. But it is up to you to earn the face you have at fifty.

—Coco Chanel

Glamour is just **sex** that got **civilized.**

—Dorothy Lamour

I have no regrets. Regrets only makes wrinkles.

—Sophia Loren

I'll use science to help nature if that's what I feel like.

—Brigitte Nielsen

Any girl can be glamorous.
All you have to do is **stand still**
and **look stupid.**

—Hedy Lamarr

*I feel **more naked** with makeup on
than I do **without it.***

—Brooke Shields

CHAPTER 2

She's All That

ONCE UPON A TIME in a land not so far away, women were often referred to as the weaker sex, short-changed at the workplace, oppressed by silly laws, chastised for being in touch with their emotions, and generally under-appreciated and underestimated. Still, despite the inequality and persecution, girl power has prevailed in the form of women rulers, VIPs, media darlings, CEOs, writers, scientists, athletes, scandalmongers, and all-around legends. It's worth taking a look back at the lives of those defiant divas who helped shape our world and who proved that, despite its name, *his*-tory isn't just a man's domain. Not only do women measure up to the greatest men of all time, they gave *birth* to 'em, too. If that weren't enough to convince you, just remember what Ginger Rogers said: "I did everything Fred [Astaire] did, only backwards and in high heels."

BLAME IT
ON THE REIGN

Whether rulers supreme or royal pains in the keister,
these chicks in charge left a lasting impression on
their subjects.

CATHERINE THE GREAT

You would think that she would have tipped her wigmaker a little something extra for giving her a hairpiece made of pure silver threads. Instead, this paranoid Russian empress (sometimes called "The Enlightened Despot") is said to have imprisoned the poor man in an iron cage in her bedchamber for three years!

MARIE ANTOINETTE

Uh…a little *privacy*, please? To prove that her baby was truly of royal lineage (and not switched at birth), the French queen was forced to deliver her first child in a room packed with several hundred spectators. Her labor was such a mortifying fiasco that she abolished public birth ceremonies soon thereafter.

Queen Elizabeth I

This famous sovereign owned one of the world's first flushing toilets, which was invented for her by her godson in 1596. No wonder it's called the "throne!"

Cleopatra

Just call her the Estée Lauder of the ancient Nile Valley. This Egyptian queen bathed in asses' milk daily for a radiant complexion, created red lip pigment from crushed beetles and ant eggs, and concocted a hair tonic from burnt mice and horse teeth in an attempt to cure her beloved Caesar's male pattern baldness.

Queen Juana

Devastated by the death of her husband, this Spanish monarch refused to bury him and took his coffin with her wherever she went, confident that he would eventually come back to life. Occasionally, Juana opened the coffin to gaze lovingly at her late spouse's decomposing remains, thereby earning the eminently suitable nickname "La Loca."

TSARINA ALEXANDRA

When a sexually depraved monk named Grigory Rasputin claimed that he had magical powers that could heal her hemophiliac son, this regal Russian bought his promises. Believing God spoke to her through this holy man, she also allowed him to weigh in on affairs of state, which eventually led to the demise of her family's dynasty. The moral? Never trust an evil-eyed sex fiend.

CATHERINE DE' MEDICI

Thin was in for this haughty French queen, who decreed that the ideal waist size for ladies in her court was a mere thirteen inches. She introduced a steel corset (or as some might say, torture device) to help her subjects acquire such measurements in a cinch.

EMPRESS JOSEPHINE

When new hubby, Napoleon, refused to let her favorite pug sleep in their conjugal bed, Josephine delivered an ultimatum: If her pooch couldn't stay in the bed, neither would she. Needless to say, her shortie spouse relented, but we assume that he drew the line with Jo's other pet: a camisole-wearing orangutan that had been trained to curtsy!

Queen Victoria

Crown jewels are great and all, but when it comes to memorable royal gifts, nothing beats the musical bustle commissioned for this venerable monarch's Golden Jubilee. It played a rousing rendition of "God Save the Queen" whenever the ruler sat down.

Empress Theodora

The ancient Byzantine paparazzi must have had a field day when Emperor Justinian married this former prostitute and circus performer. Despite her scandalous past, her husband regarded her as a full partner on the throne, letting her pass pro-women laws including mandating the death penalty for rapists and enabling ladies to inherit property.

Queen Ranavalona

Known as the "Caligula of Madagascar," this cruel queen executed one million of her own subjects including Christians, most of her relatives, and any person who had the misfortune of appearing in her dreams.

Mary, Queen of Scots

Generally recognized as the first female golfer, this Scottish tyrant (who was actually French) is believed to have coined the term "caddy" after calling her assistants on the green "cadets." During her reign, she perfected her swing on the links at St. Andrews, one of the world's earliest golf courses.

Elizabeth Báthory

Nicknamed "The Blood Countess," this noblewoman of Romania was responsible for the torture and death of hundreds of young servant girls, whose blood she allegedly bathed in with the belief that it would keep her complexion wrinkle-free.

EYEBROW RAISERS

Nothing can seal a gal's place in history like raising a ruckus, stirring up scandal, or generally launching one's own "shock and awe" campaign. Here's how these little misses made jaws drop.

MATA HARI

During WWI, this Dutch exotic dancer (with a weakness for men in uniform) used her art of seduction to spy for Germans, scoring military secrets between the sheets. Alas, her lusty allure couldn't ultimately save her from the firing squad when her double-crossing dalliances were discovered.

SARAH BERNHARDT

This famous French actress's eccentricities included occasionally sleeping in a coffin that she acquired after a doctor informed her (mistakenly, as it turns out) that she didn't have long to live. Preoccupied with death from that point on, she kept the casket in her bedroom, and when guests came to visit, she was even known to serve tea on it.

ANNIE OAKLEY

This famous female sharp shooter had such precise aim with her rifle that she once shot the ashes off the cigarette held between the lips of the Prince of Prussia, thereby earning kudos for not making this VIP an R.I.P.

MARCHESA LUISA CASATI

This kooky Italian fashionista of the early 20th century knew how to accessorize. She would walk around town with snakes (both live and stuffed) entwined around her body and pet cheetahs on jeweled leashes. On one infamous occasion, she attended the ballet with fresh chicken blood dripping down her arm. A trendsetter? Not so much.

POPE JOAN

Legend has it that a woman disguised herself as a man and served as pope for two years in the 9th century. The imposter ended up blowing her cover, big time, by giving birth on a public thoroughfare during a papal procession in front of astonished bystanders, who undoubtedly murmured something to the effect of, "Holy &#%!?@!"

PHRYNE

This ancient Greek prostitute, while on trial for heresy, managed to prompt an acquittal by flashing her bare breasts for the all-male jury. Justice, it would appear, isn't so blind after all!

LUCREZIA BORGIA

To accept a dinner invite from this notorious Italian blueblood was a risky move considering her dining companions occasionally didn't survive the meal. It's alleged that she offed them with drops of poison administered from a secret compartment in her ring.

MARY MALLON

After infecting countless people with typhoid fever, this Irish American cook evaded health officials for five years and continued to work in kitchens in spite of her deadly contagion, thus sparking a devastating epidemic. When authorities finally caught up with her, she allegedly threatened them with a carving fork before ultimately being locked up in a sanitarium for the rest of her days.

AGAINST ALL ODDS

*Naysayers and obstacles be damned, these women rose to
the occasion, leaving the rest of the world exclaiming,
"Not bad—for a girl."*

BARBARA WALTERS

She might have cowered off to the confines of print journalism after
legendary television news producer Don Hewitt remarked, "With your
voice, nobody is going to let you broadcast!"

BETSY ROSS

Sure, she is credited with sewing the first official American flag, but the
seamstress has another equally impressive distinction: She is the only
living woman ever to have inspired a Pez dispenser!

SOPHIE GERMAIN

When this young Frenchwoman developed a passion for numbers, her parents (who didn't want a math geek on their hands) kept her bedroom pitch black at night to prevent her from studying. Undeterred, the mademoiselle continued her education at an all-male academy, posing as a mysterious male student. She eventually devised a mathematic formula that made it feasible to build skyscrapers.

LISA MEITNER

As if nuclear physics weren't tough enough, this scientific pioneer also had to fight the field's rampant chauvinism. After delivering a lecture on "The Significance of Radioactivity for Cosmic Processes," she was later cited in the academic press as an expert on "cosmetic" physics.

COCO CHANEL

Never let a bad hair day get you down. When a gas heater explosion at the Paris Ritz hotel left her long dark locks covered in grime and soot, this fashion icon chopped off her tresses, thus creating an instant new trend among flappers of the era: the bob. She followed "suit" as a designer by raising hemlines and doing away with confining stays and corsets. For that, we all breathe a little easier.

SACAJAWEA

Typical men, Lewis and Clark needed help with directions on their expedition across America and turned to this fifteen-year-old Shoshone Indian to help. Not only did she endure all the same hardships as the guys, she did it all with an infant strapped to her back! Today, there are more statues in her honor than any other woman in American history.

ABIGAIL ADAMS

While the White House was under its initial construction, this ever-resourceful first lady decided that the East Room, still lacking a roof, was a convenient place to hang a clothesline so as not to air the president's dirty laundry before the public eye! Some claim that her ghost (clutching a laundry basket) still haunts the room.

ELIZABETH VAN LEW

A lifelong abolitionist, this Southern belle spied on the Confederacy by pretending to be senile. Walking the streets in tattered clothes and talking to herself, her guise ensured that no one would suspect her. She smuggled her secret missives on onionskin, which she slipped through pinpricks into hollowed-out eggshells.

Julia Child

Before becoming a renowned chef, cookbook author, and television host, Child whipped up a recipe for shark repellant while working as an employee at the Office of Strategic Services during WWII. Her creation kept Jaws and friends at bay so that submerged explosives could reach their intended target—German U-boats.

A NOVEL APPROACH

Although their lives weren't always an open book, here are some little-known facts about famous literary ladies.

JANE AUSTEN

We would have known her by the unfortunate name of Mrs. Jane Bigg-Wither had she not backed-out of an engagement to a wealthy man named Harris Bigg-Wither. She initially accepted his proposal, only to change her mind on the following day.

MARGARET MITCHELL

Thank goodness for rewrites! In her early draft of *Gone with the Wind*, the author dubbed her heroine not Scarlett, but Pansy O'Hara, while the plantation house, Tara, went by the much more fussy Fountenoy Hall.

J. K. ROWLING

Joanne Kathleen Rowling's British publisher, Bloomsbury, opted for this pseudonym lest girl-wary young boys wouldn't want to read her "Harry Potter" books. The author was practically penniless when she started writing the first book in the series on a stalled train and was living on the British equivalent of welfare. She is now the richest woman in England.

ANNE FRANK

Upon first reading the young Holocaust victim's newly discovered diary, one New York publisher remarked: "The girl doesn't have a special perception or feeling which will lift that book above the curiosity level." More than twenty-five million copies of her journal have since been sold, making it one of the best-selling books of all time.

MARY SHELLEY

She wrote her classic monster tale, *Frankenstein*, while vacationing in Lake Geneva with her husband, Percy Bysshe Shelley, and Lord Byron after they had challenged each other to a ghost-story competition as a way of waiting out horrid weather. Had the sun been shining, her masterpiece might never have materialized.

AGATHA CHRISTIE

Known as the "Duchess of Death," the most successful mystery writer of all time never attended school because her mother believed it would destroy her brain and ruin her eyes. While working as a WWI Red Cross nurse, she learned about prescriptions and poisons, which would later factor heavily into her plots.

COLETTE

This French writer's wild life offered plenty of inspiration for her provocative novels. After divorcing her philandering first husband, she took up with a cross-dressing lesbian and performed bawdy acts at the Moulin Rouge. After marrying her second husband, she had an affair with her stepson, which she then wrote about in a subsequent novel. "You will do foolish things," she once noted, "But do them with enthusiasm!"

EMILY DICKINSON

Although this poet's reclusive nature is legendary, her anti-social behavior didn't preclude her from befriending children in her neighborhood. She often offered them baked treats and notes in a basket that she lowered down from her bedroom window.

JOYCE CAROL OATES

Oates, who has published over one hundred volumes of poetry, fiction, and criticism, got her first "real book" (*Alice's Adventures in Wonderland*) and her first typewriter from her grandmother, Blanche, whose photo she keeps on her writing desk. Blanche also served as the inspiration for the protagonist of her novel *The Gravedigger's Daughter*.

MOTHERS OF INVENTION

Prompted by necessity, inspiration, or years of academic research, these female inventors made lasting contributions in big ways and small. We're willing to bet that at least a few of the following innovations are ones you would be loath to live without.

Windshield wipers: Mary Anderson; 1903

Automatic dishwasher: Josephine Cochrane; 1889

Disposable diaper: Marion Donovan; 1951

Kevlar: Stephanie Louise Kwolek; 1971

Liquid Paper: Bette Nesmith Graham; 1951

Chocolate chip cookies: Ruth Graves Wakefield; 1930

The Snugli baby carrier: Ann Moore; 1969

TV dinner: Betty Cronin; 1952

Scotchgard stain repellant: Patsy Sherman; 1956

Barbie doll and prosthetic breast: Ruth Handler; 1959

Nystatin anti-fungal drug: Elizabeth Lee Hazen and Rachel Fuller Brown; 1957

Closed-circuit security camera: Marie Brown; 1966

Hideaway bed: Sarah Goode; 1885

Dandruff shampoo: Josie Stuart; 1903

Lactaid: Virginia Holsinger; 1976

Laserphaco Probe for cataract treatment: Patricia Bath; 1986

Electric-powered carpet sweeper: Corinne Dufour; 1900

Machine for making brown paper bags: Margaret Knight

Frozen pizza: Rose Totino; 1979

Stove Top stuffing: Ruth Siems; 1975

Cordless phone: Terri Pall; 1965

FEMININE
FRONTRUNNERS

They'll never forget their first time, and,
as it was history-making, neither should you!

Virginia Dare—First person born in America to English parents
(1587)

Mary Katherine Goddard—First female publisher in
America (1766) with *The Providence Gazette* and probably the first to
own a bookstore (1789)

Martha Washington—First First Lady (1789)

Anne Parrish—First person to establish a charitable organization
for women in America, The House of Industry (1795)

Victoria Woodhull—First woman to run for president when she
was on the Equal Rights Party ticket with Frederick Douglass (1872)

Ellen Swallow Richards—First American woman to obtain a science degree when she graduated from M.I.T. (1873)

Mary Baker Eddy—First woman to found a major religion, Christian Science (1879)

Annie Edison Taylor—First person, a schoolteacher, to go over Niagara Falls in a barrel (1901)

Baroness Bertha von Suttner—First woman to win the Nobel Peace Prize (1905)

Harriet Quimby—First licensed female pilot (1911) and first female to fly solo across the English Channel (1912)

Opha Mae Johnson—First woman to enlist in the Marines (1918)

Edith Wharton—First woman to win a Pulitzer Prize for fiction with *The Age of Innocence* (1921)

Margaret Gorman—First Miss America (1921)

Halina Knonpacka—First woman to win an Olympic gold medal (1928)

Amelia Earhart—First woman to fly across the Atlantic (1928), solo across the Atlantic (1932), solo non-stop coast-to-coast (1932), solo from California to Hawaii (1935) and from the Red Sea to India (1937)

Hattie Wyatt Caraway—First woman elected to the U.S. Senate; from Arkansas (1932)

Lettie Pate Whitehead—First woman to serve as a director of a major corporation, The Coca-Cola Company (1934)

Hattie McDaniel—First African-American woman to win an Academy Award: Best Supporting Actress for *Gone with the Wind* (1940)

Hedy Lamarr—First woman to appear nude in a film when she starred in the Czech import, *Ecstasy* (1933)

Francesca Xavier Cabrini—First American citizen to be canonized by the Catholic Church when she was declared Patron Saint of Immigrants (1946)

Florence Chadwick—First woman to swim the English Channel in both directions (1951) and first to swim the twenty-six miles from Catalina Island to California (1952)

Valentina Vladimirovna Tereshkova—First woman, a Russian cosmonaut, in space (1963)

Patsy Takemoto Mink—First Asian-American woman elected to the U.S. Congress (1965)

Patricia Palinkas—First woman to play in a professional football game (1970)

Diane Crump—First female jockey to ride in the Kentucky Derby (1970)

Sally Jean Priesand—First woman ordained as a rabbi in the United States (1972)

Juanita Kreps—First woman director of the New York Stock Exchange (1972)

Junko Tabei—First woman to reach Mount Everest's summit (1975)

Janet Guthrie—First woman to race at the Indianapolis 500 (1977)

Sandra Day O'Connor—First gal to get a judge's gavel at the U.S. Supreme Court (1981)

Courteney Cox Arquette—First person to use the word "period" in a biological sense on U.S. TV when she did a commercial for Tampax (1985)

Wilma Mankiller—First female chief of the Cherokee Nation of Oklahoma (1985)

Dr. Antonia Novello—First woman (and first Hispanic person) sworn in as U.S. Surgeon General (1990)

Joni Mitchell—First woman to receive the Century Award, music magazine *Billboard's* highest honor (1995)

Tyra Banks—First African-American woman to pose on the covers of the *Sports Illustrated* swimsuit issue, GQ, and the Victoria's Secret catalog (All in 1996)

Ellen DeGeneres—First female comedian invited by Johnny Carson for a chat on the couch on *The Tonight Show*; Also becomes TV's first openly gay star in 1997 when she announces, "Yep, I'm Gay," on the cover of *Time*

Nancy Ruth Mace—First female cadet to graduate from the Citadel, the formerly all-male military school in South Carolina (1999)

Effa Manley—First woman elected to the Baseball Hall of Fame (2006)

Drew Gilpin Faust—First woman to be named president of Harvard in the school's 371-year history (2007)

By the Numbers

1.8

Percent chance that any woman has of going to prison in her lifetime; For men, that number jumps to 11.35 percent

10

Shoe size worn by Jacqueline Kennedy Onassis

$14

Amount Rosa Parks was fined for refusing to give up her seat at the front of the bus

18 Number of women sailing on the Mayflower when it first landed in America

18

Length, in feet, of the hair of Xie Qiuping, who holds the Guinness record for longest hair (as of 2004)

Number of women killed during the
Salem witchcraft trials of 1692

60

Number of different languages into which Harriet Beecher Stowe's novel, *Uncle Tom's Cabin*, has been translated

77

Amount in cents that U.S. women made in 2005 for every dollar earned by men

1884

Year the women's singles competition began at Wimbledon

1909

*Year International Women's Day
was first observed*

1979

Year the first Susan B. Anthony
one-dollar coin was minted

3,000

*Number of pairs of shoes former
Philippines first lady Imelda Marcos
abandoned when her family went
into exile in 1986*

563-32-0764

Marilyn Monroe's Social Security Number

Because I am a woman,
I must make unusual efforts to succeed.
If I fail, no one will say, "She doesn't have
what it takes." They will say,
"Women don't have what it takes."

—Clare Boothe Luce

I'm tough, I'm ambitious, and
I know exactly what I want.
If that makes me a bitch, okay.

—Madonna

If you want anything said, ask a man. If you want anything done, ask a woman.

—Margaret Thatcher

Well-behaved women

rarely make history.

—Laurel Thatcher Ulrich

Whatever women do they must

do twice as well as men

to be thought half as good.

Luckily, this is not difficult.

—Charlotte Whitton

If women want **any rights more than they have,** why don't they **just take them** and not be talking about it.

—Sojourner Truth

The rooster may crow,

but the hens

deliver the goods.

—Ann Richards

I'm the girl who lost her reputation
and never missed it.

—Mae West

I think it's time we voted for senators with breasts. After all, **we've been voting for boobs** long enough.

—Claire Sargent

CHAPTER 3

Retail Therapy

ANYONE WHO'S EVER fought valiantly through a "Day After Thanksgiving" sale or convinced herself that her Size 9 foot fit a sales-rack Size 8 peep toe knows that shopping is not for the faint of heart. But tragic dressing room mirrors and calamitous credit card bills are something all must face in the pursuit of sartorial success. The love of bargain-hunting, fine fabrics, and the perfect fit is so universally female that we're willing to bet that the first cave women probably asked their significant others, "Does this animal skin make me look fat?" Little has changed in that regard, although thankfully, some things (whalebone corsets and Members Only jackets), have been relegated to footnotes in fashion history. Whether you're a haute couture honey or a bargain basement broad, shopping isn't just retail therapy...it's a religion.

If the Shoe Fits...

Man cannot live on bread alone, nor can woman survive
on only one pair of shoes. Here's a brief review of our
longstanding fascination with footwear.

In 1533, Catherine de' Medici introduced
high heels to Parisians when she teetered
on a pair for her marriage to the Duke
d'Orléans. Because European working-class
women couldn't wear such impractical shoes
in their day-to-day existence, high heels
were proof of privilege.

Marie Antoinette had a servant whose "sole" purpose was to tend to the queen's five hundred pairs of slippers, which were organized by style and color.

Originally worn by male footmen in the 16th century, "pumps" take their name from the sound that they made when darting across a polished floor.

The concept of a right and left shoe originated in early 19th-century America when cobblers began differentiating between the two feet. Called "crookeds," the improvement made for a profoundly more comfortable fit.

In 1936, it would have cost you only eight hundred pennies to buy a pair of penny loafers as the preppy mainstays first retailed for eight dollars.

The original platform shoe originated in 16th century Venice and was called a chopine. Because some reached heights of twenty inches, women who wore them were usually accompanied by a servant or walked with a cane for balance. It's said that husbands preferred wives who wore chopines as it limited their movement and discouraged sinful behavior.

In the 1960s, an Illinois inventor created a high-heeled shoe with an adjustable, telescopic heel.

From Hans Christian Anderson's *The Red Shoes* to the film version of *The Wizard of Oz*, red shoes have long been imbued with a mythical aura of magic and power. Perhaps that accounts for why high-priced designer Christian Louboutin finishes off his fabulous footwear with red soles.

Mary Janes are named after a character in a popular early 1900s comic strip called *Buster Brown*. Meanwhile, Hush Puppies take their name from the balls of fried dough popular in Southern cuisine. After hearing that these breaded-treats were sometimes tossed to dogs to quiet their barking, the footwear company realized that their comfy suede shoes also soothed "barking dogs" (a.k.a. sore feet).

Rubber-soled shoes were first marketed by Keds in 1917. The brand name comes from combining the Latin term for "foot" (*ped*) and the first letter of the word for the intended wearers (kids).

Looking for a more optimal running shoe, University of Oregon track coach Bill Bowerman designed the first pair of Nikes. He later perfected the shoe's waffle-style sole in his kitchen by shaping rubber in an actual waffle iron.

THE SKINNY
ON THE SKIVVIES

They're called unmentionables in more delicate circles, but when it comes to lingerie, there's plenty worth talking about. Here's a foundation for the basic understanding of undies.

Padded bras are hardly a modern phenomenon. When women in colonial America wanted a little more doodle in their dandy, they turned to the "bosom friend," which was a garment with breast-enhancing quilted padding. In the 1950s, the far less congenial sounding "merry widow" corset helped women achieve that legendary hourglass figure.

Made from whalebone or bamboo in the early-to-mid 1800s, a corset took about a half hour to squeeze into and often required help from other ladies of the house. In the event that she had no one to tighten her laces, a woman might tie the corset strings to a bedpost and lean away to cinch herself up.

In 1851, Amelia Jenks Bloomer, deputy postmistress of that suffragettes' stronghold, Seneca Falls, New York, defied the decorum of the day and appeared in public wearing long baggy pants under her skirt. Her daring act prompted women everywhere to start wearing "bloomers," as they came to be known.

Hoop skirts and crinolines created a sensation around the time of the Civil War, but eventually proved too inconvenient to withstand the test of time. The skirts were so voluminous that it became difficult for women to pass through doorways. That, and male suitors had a hard time getting close enough to actually make a pass!

In 1914, a young American socialite named Polly Jacob needed a less bulky undergarment for her slinky new dress. She fashioned the modern brassiere using two handkerchiefs and some ribbon. She eventually sold the patent on her design to the Warner Brothers Corset Company for $1500.

When 1970s-era feminists burned their bras outside the original Frederick's of Hollywood store, owner Frederick Mellinger, who pioneered the first modern push-up bra (called The Rising Star), responded by publicly proclaiming, "The law of gravity will win out."

In 2002, Victoria's Secret sued a sex shop in Fort Knox, Kentucky, operating under the name Victor's Little Secret. The Supreme Court eventually ruled that the copycat name did not infringe on the company's trademark.

The latest technology in underwear innovation includes a product called Under-Ease, which, according to the product's Web site, contains a pocket in the back with a removable charcoal filter aimed at helping neutralize any embarrassing "malodorous flatus."

TRIED AND TRUE BLUES

From the construction site to campuses and clubs, jeans have become the world's pants of preference. Try these denim deets on for size.

Levi Strauss, the father of the modern blue jean, wasn't a designer by trade. He operated a wholesale dry goods business in San Francisco during the Gold Rush of the mid-1800s. More surprisingly, the idea that jumpstarted his denim empire wasn't his. In 1872, Reno-based tailor Jacob Davis, who bought fabric from Strauss, wrote him about his new pants-making method, which involved placing metal rivets at the points of strain (like pocket corners). The design was a hit with miners, but as Davis didn't have money for a patent, he suggested Strauss front the funds and they become partners.

Strauss and Davis were granted the patent for "Improvement in Fastening Pocket-Openings" on May 20, 1873. The first prototypes had only three pockets and were made by individual seamstresses in their home until Strauss opened a factory in the 1880s. In 1890, they added the watch pocket, and the company's signature 501 style (back then referred to as the XX) was born. The current five-pocket industry standard was established by 1905. Zippers were sewn into Levi's for the first time in 1954 after complaints poured in from Easterners unaccustomed to button flies.

Jeans were originally called waist overalls. Scholars disagree about why they became known as jeans despite being made of denim and not of the fabric called jean, which was also used to make workwear of that era. Although the two materials are very similar, denim is stronger, more expensive, and woven with a colored thread and a white thread whereas jean material employs monochromatic thread.

Wrangler parent company Blue Bell opened in 1904 and originally operated out of a church in downtown Greensboro, North Carolina.

In 1920, tiny pairs of Lee overalls were handed out at county fairs. The salesman in charge of the promotion dressed up doe-eyed dolls in leftover denim scraps and gave them to vendors. A Minneapolis store window display ignited a fad, and the company started mass-producing the hand-painted doll in hand-sewn duds. Buddy Lees originally sold for $2.50 and can now command up to $250 at auction. The mascot collection grew to include an engineer, a cowboy, and an athlete. The little guy was retired in 1960, but was reinstated as a bobblehead in 1998 and appeared in a commercial with Sarah Michelle Gellar.

Cuffs are purely a fashion statement today, but they used to serve a purpose. Cowboys stashed packs of cigarettes in the folds and used them as ashtrays when riding through flammable brush.

In the 1930s, jeans started invading college campuses. Sophomores at U.C. Berkeley and the University of Oregon claimed the casual garment as their own, forbidding freshmen to wear them.

Crane & Co., a firm that makes
paper on which money
is printed, uses pulped denim
remnants in its recipe.
The scraps make up between
twenty to thirty percent
of each bill.

Before the advent of pre-shrunk fabric and chemical processes, wearers would submerge themselves in water for a few hours to shrink the fabric to their own body and achieve a more comfortable fit. John Wayne bundled up new blues, threw them off the Catalina Island pier, and let them soak in the sea for a few days before the start of each cowboy flick that helped make him and his pants legendary. Wanting Marlon Brando's jeans to fit snugly in the 1947 Broadway run of *A Streetcar Named Desire*, the show's costumer fitted and pinned the actor's pants while they were soaking wet, then ran them through a washing machine for twenty-four hours.

Jeans can practically pass for formal wear today, but there was a time when the iconic fashion statement had serious image problems. For example, crooner Bing Crosby tried to check into a ritzy hotel while on a hunting trip in Canada and was turned away because he was sporting dungarees. In the '50s, several U.S. schools banned jeans because they were associated with bad boys like James Dean, who donned denim in *Rebel Without a Cause*.

In 1954, a pair of J.C. Penney's Foremost jeans came with a price tag of $2.29. Almost four decades later, Tommy Hilfiger paid $37,000 for three pairs of Foremosts worn by Marilyn Monroe in *River of No Return*. He hung one in his office and gifted another to Britney Spears.

Vogue editor Anna Wintour isn't too much of a fashionista to appreciate stonewash. When she took over the reigns of the magazine in 1988, her first cover featured a model in a Christian Lacroix bejeweled top and a pedestrian pair of Guess jeans.

Brooke Shields was paid $500,000 to appear in her famous series of Calvin Klein commercials shot by acclaimed fashion photographer Richard Avedon. Ironically, one of the taglines she seductively recited was, "Whenever I get some money, I buy Calvins. And if there's any left, I pay the rent."

Levi Strauss & Co. paid $46,532 to buy back a pair of its own jeans on eBay in May 2001. The jeans, which were found in a Nevada mining town and dated back to the 1880s, were considered priceless and one-of-a-kind and are now in the company's archives.

Jordache was founded by three brothers from Tel Aviv in the late '70s. The oldest sibling arrived in America with only twenty-five dollars to his name. After his brothers joined him, they opened a store in Brooklyn, which was looted during a blackout. They turned lemons into lemonade using the insurance settlement as seed money to begin manufacturing the future bestsellers.

When *Forbes* put together a
"Most Expensive Jeans" list in 2005,
a pair adorned with Swarovski
crystals from Escada's couture line
topped the tally. They started at
$7,500 and had no price cap,
although the costliest pair they
had made at the time cost
ten thousand dollars.

Some high-end designers wished blue jeans had been their brainstorm. Yves Saint Laurent, often credited as the first to bring blue jeans to the haute couture runway, said, "I wish I had invented [them]. They have expression, modesty, sex appeal, simplicity—all I hope for in my clothes." Bill Blass decreed Levi's, "the best single item of apparel ever designed." And couturier Charles James summed it up, "Denim is America's gift to the world." But not everyone who was anyone thought jeans were a good idea. Mormon leader Brigham Young balked when buttons were first added to the front of pants in the 1800s labeling them "fornication pants."

Trendy jean designer Adriano Goldschmied's

initial dream was to become a pro skier,

but his mother didn't exactly approve of that

career path. To keep her off his back, he opened

a boutique in the Italian Alps in 1972 and

experimented with clothing design despite a

total lack of experience or schooling.

It's a Mall World

Minnesota's Mall of America, the nation's largest retail and entertainment complex, opened in August 1992. Below we talk shop (and stats) about this capital of consumerism.

To put its colossal 4.2-million square feet into perspective, consider what fits inside: 258 Statues of Liberty lying down, thirty-two Boeing 747s, seven Yankee Stadiums, and all four heads on Mount Rushmore.

While it isn't the world's biggest shopping center, it is the most-visited mall on the planet. More than forty million people step inside this shopper's paradise annually, which is more than the attendance at Graceland and the Grand Canyon combined. About four out of every ten MOA customers live outside a 150-mile radius of the site. One draw: there's no sales tax on clothing.

There are more than 520 stores in this mondo-mall. If a shopper spent ten minutes browsing at every store, it would take more than eighty-six hours to complete the visit. As it is, the average patron stays for eighty minutes and spends about seventy-five dollars.

The mall employs eleven thousand people year-round, and that number rises to thirteen thousand during summers and holidays. It contributes more than $1.8 billion per year to Minnesota's economy.

*Any old mall can have stores and restaurants,
so MOA ups the ante with a fourteen-screen movie
theater, the country's largest indoor amusement park,
a 1.2 million gallon walk-through aquarium, a four-
story LEGO Imagination Center, a NASCAR-themed
speedway, Dinosaur Walk Museum, flight simulator,
and the first-ever college campus in a mall.*

After you register for china and stemware at MOA,
you can hold the wedding ceremony there as well.
More than four thousand couples have exchanged
vows in its Chapel of Love.

This cathedral to capitalism was built on the former site of Metropolitan Stadium, where the Minnesota Vikings and Minnesota Twins played until 1982. To honor the location's pro-ball past, a plaque in the amusement park commemorates the former location of home plate. Additionally, one stadium seat was placed at the exact location (including elevation) where it would have been found when Hall of Famer Harmon Killebrew hit a 520-foot home run on June 3, 1967.

Despite the state's extreme temperature swings, the weather inside the structure is always a perfect seventy degrees.

MOA made big-screen cameos in *The Mighty Ducks* and *Jingle All the Way*. It hosted the premiere of *Ice Age* and the Turner Network debut of *WWE's Monday Nitro* wrestling competition. *The Today Show* aired live from MOA in 2002 with a performance by Mariah Carey. The Travel Channel and the Discovery Channel have both aired documentaries about its hallowed halls.

By the Numbers

25

Number of pounds the first laptops to hit the market weighed

30

Average number of shoes owned by an American woman, according to *Shoes: A Celebration of Pumps, Sandals, Slippers & More* by Linda O'Keefe

35

Minutes it took for the final sailing of the Queen Elizabeth 2 luxury liner to sell out

40DD

Dolly Parton's bra size

50

Percent of the $20 billion annual toy sales that occur between October and December

60 Percent of household bills wives are in charge of paying, according to *The Journal of Socio-Economics*

94

Percent of home furnishing purchases in which women are the central decision maker. It drops to 60 percent for vehicle purchases.

3,500

Number of accessories on display at
Amsterdam's Museum of Bags and Purses

8,061

Number of diamonds used on Damien Hirst's "For the Love of God" skull art, which sold for $100 million—a record price for a work sold by a living artist

$12,000

What the first digital cameras retailed for

$21,150

What Madonna's infamous conical Blonde Ambition Tour bra, designed by Jean-Paul Gaultier, fetched at auction in 2001

500,000 to 750,000

Estimated number of iPhones sold the first week the Apple gadget was available in the United States

1.7 million

Number of hits received for the eBay auction for a grilled cheese sandwich allegedly bearing the Virgin Mary's likeness in the char; It eventually sold to Internet casino GoldenPalace.com for $28,000

$11 million

Value of the jewel-encrusted
Victoria's Secret "Fantasy Bra"
worn by Heidi Klum in a 2003
televised fashion show

40 million

Number of original Furbys sold during
the toy's initial three-year run

$29.15 billion

Total amount of lingerie sales in
the United States every year

Brevity is the soul of lingerie.

—Dorothy Parker

One quarter of what you buy will turn out to be **mistakes.**

—Delia Ephron

You'd be surprised *at how much it costs* to look this cheap.

—Dolly Parton

Nothing that costs only a dollar is worth having.

—Elizabeth Arden

I only put clothes on **so that I'm not naked** when I go out shopping.

—Julia Roberts

Don't ever wear artistic jewelry;
it wrecks a woman's reputation.

—Colette

Women in skirts should keep their knees together,

not just for modesty but out of politeness,

since few people really want a view of

the undergarments of women

sitting across from them.

—Peggy Post

What woman doesn't spend
ninety percent of her life
going in and out of the closet?

—Donna Karan

I'd much rather be a woman than a man. Women can cry, they can wear cute clothes, and they're the first to be rescued off sinking ships.

—Gilda Radner

CHAPTER 4

Love and Marriage

AH, LOVE AND MARRIAGE. It's just like Ol' Blue Eyes used to sing. Of course, anyone who's ever ridden in a horse-drawn carriage can tell you that the ride is as bumpy as it is thrilling. The subject of romance has spawned some of the greatest literature of all time as well as some of the cheesiest rock 'n' roll ballads. It can also leave us singing the blues. Yet every day, women get weak-in-the-knees over a first crush or dream about finding "happily ever after" with Brad Pitt's long-lost twin. Love is powerful stuff. It can turn the most obstinate bachelor into a family man and prompt even the most stalwart among us to tear up at maudlin greeting card commercials. Cynical singletons may (sometimes, quite rightfully) mock love's gushy sentimentality, but one prick of Cupid's arrow and they, too, will be basking in the glory of love before you can say *amor vincit omnia.* (Love conquers all.)

BUDGET-BUSTING BETROTHALS

The sky's often the limit when power-list pairs plan a walk down the aisle. But the following twenty couples took "for richer" to a whole new level, and their lavish choices landed them on Forbes' first-ever "Most Expensive Celebrity Weddings" list in 2007. Unfortunately even superstars can't buy everlasting love. Nearly half of the couples on this roster have since split.

The Couple: Elizabeth Hurley and Arun Nayar

Wedding Date: March 2007

Estimated Cost: $2.5 million

Big Splurges: Double ceremonies and activities that spanned eight days in two countries (Sudeley Castle in England and Umaid Bhawan Palace in India, where suites cost as much as ten thousand dollars a night); a chiffon gown designed by Donatella Versace

The Couple: Tom Cruise and Katie Holmes

Wedding Date: November 2006

Estimated Cost: $2 million

Big Splurges: Italy's 15th-century Odescalchi Castle; all attire personally designed by Giorgio Armani; five-tiered chocolate cake with marzipan roses; a week's worth of pre-wedding activities

The Couple: Nicole Kidman and Keith Urban

Wedding Date: June 2006

Estimated Cost: $250,000

Big Splurges: Cream Rolls-Royce limo; Balenciaga gown; performances by both Urban and Hugh Jackman at the reception for the two hundred guests

The Couple: Elton John and David Furnish

Wedding Date: December 2005

Estimated Cost: $1.5 million

Big Splurges: Exchanged diamond wedding bands at Windsor's Guildhall (also site of Prince Charles and Camilla Parker Bowles nuptials); vintage pink champagne; two heated tents massive enough to house six hundred guests

The Couple: Christina Aguilera and Jordan Bratman

Wedding Date: November 2005

Estimated Cost: $2 million

Big Splurges: Two designer dresses; a winter-themed tent embellished with roses, silver drapery, and dangling crystals at Napa Valley's Staglin Family Vineyard; couple booked $3,500-a-night cottage at the Auberge du Soleil

The Couple: Donald Trump and Melania Knauss

Wedding Date: January 2005

Estimated Cost: $1 million

Big Splurges: Upscale "floral designer" Preston Bailey, whose fees typically begin at $100,000; a Christian Dior gown made from three hundred feet of satin, beaded with fifteen hundred crystals, and finished with a thirteen-foot, fifty-pound train; a thirty-six-piece orchestra; four hundred guests; catered by top chef Jean-Georges Vongerichten at Trump's Palm Beach palace

The Couple: Tiger Woods and Elin Nordegren

Wedding Date: October 2004

Estimated Cost: $1.5 million

Big Splurges: Rented out entire Shady Lane Resort and hired only helicopter charter company in Barbados to ensure privacy; custom white-netted, rose-decorated pagoda for vow exchange; performance by Hootie & the Blowfish

The Couple: Tori Spelling and Charlie Shanian
Wedding Date: July 2004
Estimated Cost: $1 million
Big Splurges: Platinum floral headband inspired by the *Great Gatsby* theme; a Badgley Mischka crystal-beaded gown; Wolfgang Puck-catered meal for four hundred guests that included herb-crusted rack of lamb (We assume she got to use her parents' 56,000-square-foot Bel Air spread for free.)

The Couple: Paul McCartney and Heather Mills
Wedding Date: June 2002
Estimated Cost: $3 million
Big Splurges: Destination wedding in Ireland; a covered walkway built to shield three hundred guests from the rain as they walked to a lakeside tent for an Indian-themed party complete with authentically dressed dancers, a vegetarian feast and fireworks

The Couple: Marc Anthony and Miss Universe Dayanara Torres
Wedding Date: May 2002 (Actually, this was their vow renewal revelry.)
Estimated Cost: $500,000
Big Splurges: San Juan Cathedral in Puerto Rico; crystal-and pearl-embroidered satin Reem Acra dress; reception at the *Cuartel de Ballajá,* a Spanish garrison built in 1854 that is usually an off-limits venue

The Couple: Liza Minnelli and David Gest
Wedding Date: March 2002
Estimated Cost: $3.5 million
Big Splurges: Tony Bennett concert backed by a sixty-piece orchestra; Natalie Cole sang "Unforgettable"; twelve-tier cake and personalized favors in satin candy boxes embossed "Liza and David 4 Ever"

The Couple: Ashley Judd and Indy 500 winner Dario Franchitti
Wedding Date: December 2001
Estimated Cost: $750,000
Big Splurges: Skibo Castle in Scotland; industrial heaters for the giant reception tent; full-length beaded lace coat by Armani

The Couple: Pierce Brosnan and Keely Shaye Smith
Wedding Date: August 2001
Estimated Cost: $1.5 million
Big Splurges: Rented 13th century Ballintubber Abbey in Ireland for ceremony and lakeside Ashford Castle for reception; six-tier carrot cake modeled after Kennedy-Onassis wedding cake; ice sculpture of Rodin's *The Kiss* was groom's gift

The Couple: Madonna and Guy Ritchie
Wedding Date: December 2000
Estimated Cost: $1.5 million
Big Splurges: Custom Stella McCartney silk number topped off with a 1910 diamond tiara once worn by Princess Grace of Monaco; booked all twenty-one rooms of Scotland's Skibo Castle for guests; converted "basement" into a disco for all-night dance session

The Couple: Michael Douglas and Catherine Zeta-Jones

Wedding Date: November 2000

Estimated Cost: $1.5 million

Big Splurges: Hologram-embedded invitations to prevent crashers; Plaza Hotel location; antique Chantilly lace Christian Lacroix dress and tiara; entertainment by Bonnie Tyler and Simply Red's Mick Hucknall

The Couple: Brad Pitt and Jennifer Aniston

Wedding Date: July 2000

Estimated Cost: $1 million

Big Splurges: Suede Manolo Blahnik sandals; fifty thousand flowers (and almost as many candles) to create "Zen garden look"; fireworks over Malibu estate

The Couple: David and Victoria Beckham

Wedding Date: July 1999

Estimated Cost: $800,000

Big Splurges: Luttrellstown Castle near Dublin; Posh Spice's gold diamond-encrusted crown; trumpeters who welcomed the two hundred fifty guests; fireworks; performance by Elton John

The Couple: Mariah Carey and Tommy Mottola
Wedding Date: June 1993
Estimated Cost: $500,000
Big Splurges: Tony Fifth Avenue Church; 50 flower girls; Vera Wang dress with twenty-seven-foot-long train; diamond tiara and rhinestone-sprinkled veil; three hundred guests

The Couple: Eddie Murphy and Nicole Mitchell
Wedding Date: March 1993
Estimated Cost: $1.5 million
Big Splurges: Re-carpeted NYC's Plaza Hotel Grand Ballroom in white for ceremony and then reset the room as a disco; five hundred guests; twelve-foot dress train

The Couple: Elizabeth Taylor and Larry Fortensky
Wedding Date: October 1991
Estimated Cost: $2 million
Big Splurges: Held at Michael Jackson's Neverland Ranch with 150 guests in attendance; a yellow Valentino number proved Liz had the sagacity not to wear white for her seventh waltz down the aisle

My Funny Valentine

Whether February 14th fills your heart with dread or makes it go all pitter-patter with excitement, Valentine's Day is more than just an excuse for gorging on chocolate. Here's a little truth behind Cupid's celebration.

In the Middle Ages, one Valentine's tradition involved young men and women drawing names to determine who their Valentine would be for a week. They would wear the person's name on their sleeve, thus inspiring the expression, "Wearing one's heart on one's sleeve."

It probably comes as no big surprise that Valentine's Day has its origins in a very lusty pagan fertility celebration, Lupercalia, which the Christians eventually re-imagined (and seriously tamed down) to honor St. Valentine. Scholars still debate which of three early Christian martyrs named Valentine the holiday commemorates, but the generally accepted theory is that it's a Roman priest who may have secretly helped soldiers tie the knot. Because Emperor Claudius II had forbidden his soldiers from marrying, this was a major no-no, and Valentine was ultimately sentenced to death. Legend also claims that before he was executed, Valentine fell in love with the jailer's daughter and sent her a love letter (a.k.a., the world's first Valentine note) from his cell.

Where's the love? Not on the modern church calendar, at least not where this holiday is concerned. In 1969, the Catholic Church revised its liturgical calendar and axed any saints' feast days with sketchy historical origins, including that of St. Valentine. With no religious obligations on Valentine's Day, it's safe to say young lovers have found other ways to, er, occupy their time.

According to the U.S. Census Bureau, 180 million cards are exchanged every year on Valentine's Day, making it the second most-popular greeting card-giving occasion (Christmas ranks first.) Valentine's cards were generally homemade numbers until the 1850s when Esther A. Howland of Worcester, Massachusetts, decided to mass-produce them. Considering about one-quarter of all cards sent each year are Valentines, we're guessing Hallmark owes Esther a serious debt of gratitude. (Do they make a card for that?)

Anyone who's taken Anatomy 101 can tell you that a Valentine heart bears about as much resemblance to an actual human heart as a pineapple resembles a moray eel. So where does the shape come from? Ancient Sumerian cuneiform script features a similar shape that is a symbol for "woman." Some academics feel today's heart shape is meant to signify an entirely different part of the female anatomy. Still others think it's meant to depict the seed of the now extinct silphium fruit, or, wings, which signified the Greek goddess of love, Aphrodite.

Thank Britain's John Cadbury for introducing the first box of chocolates in 1868, which featured a depiction of the confectioner's daughter with a kitten. He later devised the now ubiquitous heart-shaped box. Meanwhile, in America, the Whitman's Sampler was the first box of candy to have its own map of filling flavors, thereby taking the guesswork out of gluttony.

The red rose (a symbol of true love) is by far the most popular flower given on Valentine's Day, but be forewarned if you receive a bouquet of yellow carnations: They traditionally signify rejection and disdain! Here are some other meanings for flowers:

Black-eyed Susan: Encouragement

Calla Lily: Majestic beauty

Daisy: Innocence

Gardenia: Secret love

Hydrangea: Vanity

Iris: Valor

Lily of the Valley: Purity, sweetness

Lotus: Mystery

Magnolia: Dignity

Peony: Healing

Petunia: Anger and resentment

LOVE 'EM AND LEAVE 'EM

So much for "'Till death do us part." Some celebrity couples can't even make it home from Vegas before calling it quits. This guide highlights the shortest matrimonial missteps of the rich and famous.

The Couple: Jennifer Lopez and Cris Judd

Marriage Length: Eight months, from October 2001 to July 2002

Breakup Backstory: Ironically, she met the choreographer on her video for "Love Don't Cost a Thing." No details on the financial settlement were reported, but a statement released by their lawyers described the resolution as "extremely amicable" and that they would "remain friends." J. Lo's first marriage (to Ojani Noa in 1997) only fared slightly better at thirteen months. But her luck seems to be changing. She has been married to singer and *El Cantante* costar Marc Anthony since June 5, 2004. They married in her Beverly Hills backyard four days after his divorce was finalized.

The Couple: Shannen Doherty and Ashley Hamilton

Marriage Length: Six months, from September 1993 to February 1994

Breakup Backstory: The *Beverly Hills, 90210* ball buster does not have a charmed love life. After her short-lived marital mess with George Hamilton's son, she gave an encore bridal performance in 2002 for nine months with Richard Salomon (the Paris Hilton sex tape's leading man). She eventually used her expertise on a 2006 reality show called *Breaking Up with Shannen Doherty*.

The Couple: Charlie Sheen and model Donna Peele

Marriage Length: Five months, from September 1995 to February 1996

Breakup Backstory: The split came hot on the heels of the Brat Packer's 30th birthday betrothal in Malibu. He since married, separated, made up with, and then divorced Denise Richards between June 2002 and November 2006 and then announced his engagement to another aspiring actress, Brooke Allen, in summer '07. Guess ex-fiancée Kelly Preston dodged a figurative bullet when she dumped him after he accidentally/literally shot her in the arm.

The Couple: Renée Zellweger and Kenny Chesney
Marriage Length: Four months in 2005
Breakup Backstory: They legally bound their love while barefoot on the beach in the U.S. Virgin Islands in May, and she filed for an annulment in September, citing "fraud," which she later said was, "simply legal language and not a reflection of Kenny's character."

The Couple: Colin Farrell and *Quills*' Amelia Warner
Marriage Length: Four months in 2001
Breakup Backstory: Maybe eloping stars should steer clear of sand. These two wed on a Tahitian island in July and he tattooed her nickname, Millie, around his ring finger. He later told GQ, "I was madly in love. There was a time I thought I'd spend the rest of my life with this girl. That time didn't last that long."

The Couple: Nicolas Cage and Lisa Marie Presley
Marriage Length: Three months and fifteen days in 2002
Breakup Backstory: Elvis's daughter and the actor who sang The King's tunes in *Wild at Heart* married after a yearlong courtship in Hawaii. Irreconcilable differences were the culprit once again. Her statement: "We shouldn't have been married in the first place. It was

a big mistake." Shocking, considering she held out for twenty months after getting hitched to headline maker Michael Jackson in May 1994.

The Couple: Pamela Anderson and Kid Rock
Marriage Length: Less than four months in 2006
Breakup Backstory: They almost had a wedding for each month of marriage, holding ceremonies in France, Tennessee, and Beverly Hills.

The Couple: Ernest Borgnine and Ethel Merman
Marriage Length: Thirty-two days
Breakup Backstory: The thrice-wed Broadway belter married twice-wed Borgnine in 1964. Their marriage was dissolved slightly more than a month later because, according to Borgnine, she was jealous of his fame and he got more fan attention while honeymooning. In her 1978 autobiography, the chapter devoted to the nuptials consisted of one blank page.

The Couple: Drew Barrymore and Jeremy Thomas
Marriage Length: Thirty days, from March to April 1994
Breakup Backstory: He was a bar owner and she was a party girl when they married after a six-week fling. She could actually make

the list twice as her union to comedian Tom Green lasted just five months in 2001. Coincidentally, *Irreconcilable Differences* is the title of one of her past projects.

The Couple: Dennis Rodman and Carmen Electra
Marriage Length: Nine days in November 1998
Breakup Backstory: Another Sin City separation. The basketball bad boy threatened annulment a little more than a week after the big day and the *Baywatch* babe filed officially the following April. A brief reconnection in 1999 ended with a judge's order to stay five hundred feet apart after a nasty hotel room spat left her with a swollen lip and him with torn threads.

The Couple: Dennis Hopper and Michelle Phillips
Marriage Length: Eight days, from Oct. 31 to Nov. 8, 1998
Breakup Backstory: Apparently, The Mamas & the Papas singer looks back fondly on her short stint as Mrs. Hopper. She said in her Lifetime special, "I will say this about Dennis Hopper: We were married for eight days, and truly, they were the happiest days of my life."

The Couple: Britney Spears and Jason Alexander

Marriage Length: Fifty-five hours in January 2004

Breakup Backstory: She and her childhood pal (not to be confused with the *Seinfeld* alum) sealed the deal at the Little White Wedding Chapel in Las Vegas a little after 5 a.m. The bride was escorted down the aisle in a baseball cap and torn jeans by a limo driver. She filed for an annulment less than three days later citing incompatibility. No one was surprised to see her hit divorce court, baby, one more time, when her second marriage to Kevin Federline disintegrated after two years and two kids in late 2006. She followed up her filing with a series of bizarre public outings (shaving her head, attacking a photographer with an umbrella, going commando at a club) and stints in rehab.

The Couple: Robin Givens and Svetozar Marinkovic

Marriage Length: One day in 1997

Breakup Backstory: Maybe she should find a nice doctor instead of plucking partners from the sports section. Marinkovic was her tennis instructor, and her eleven-month marriage to boxer Mike Tyson ended on Valentine's Day in 1989 amid claims of spousal abuse.

A MODEST PROPOSAL

Few things are more steeped in tradition than a wedding. From the bride's bouquet to the clattering cans hanging off the getaway car, we examine the where, when, and why of marriage customs and superstitions.

The tradition of wearing a white gown started with Queen Victoria's wedding to Prince Albert in 1840. Prior to that, white gowns weren't necessarily the norm. In the 16th century, brides wore gowns in any color but green, which was though to auger bad luck. Other bad luck for brides: A pig, hare, or lizard running across your path, or seeing an open grave. (Uh…something tells us you've got bigger problems to worry about if the latter comes to fruition!)

Good omens on your wedding day include rain, seeing a rainbow, sunshine (Guess they're covering their bases!), meeting a black cat, or bumping into a chimney sweep. In the not-so-fun category, pinching the bride is supposed to bring luck, as is finding a spider in the wedding dress!

You may think good weather is the reason that so many couples choose to marry in June, but the practice first began with the ancient Romans, who believed that the goddess Juno blessed any marriages that fell in her month. They also studied pig entrails to determine the best day for planning the shindig—wonder why *that* lovely practice didn't survive the test of time?

Darn those infernal evil spirits! In medieval times, a bride's bouquet was made of garlic, chives, rosemary, bay leaves, or other pungent herbs to keep bad mojo away. Today, cans tied to a couple's car bumper are supposed to offer the same sort of protection. Matching (sometimes hideous) bridesmaids' gowns, meanwhile, are meant to confuse and distract any evil spirit hoping to make away with the bride, who veils her face for extra protection.

Czech wedding guests throw peas, not rice, at the newlyweds. Girl Scouts founder Juliette Gordon Low, meanwhile, found the whole rice-throwing tradition to be not-so-auspicious when a piece of rice lodged in her good ear (she was already deaf in one) as she was leaving her wedding. The wayward grain caused an infection and prompted her to go completely deaf!

Perhaps confusing their wedding day for another famous holiday, Finnish brides traditionally went door-to-door collecting wedding gifts in a pillowcase.

The truly superstitious bride will marry on the half hour (not the top of the hour) to ensure that the hands of the clock are on their way up, not down. It's also said that the first spouse to fall asleep on their wedding night will be the first to die.

Always a bridesmaid, but never a bride. This famously defeatest dig at romantic also-rans derives from a 1923 ad for Listerine mouthwash, which suggested that just maybe, girls who were missing out on marriage might be suffering from a bout of the dragon breath. The original ad was so successful that it continued to run for many years after and was listed as No. 48 on *Ad Age* magazine's "Top 100 Advertising Campaigns of the Century."

BY THE NUMBERS

3

Percent of the 4,000 mammal species that are monogamous (And, no, homo sapiens don't make the list that includes beavers, otters, bats, and some foxes!)

9

Average number of sexual partners people have had, according to a global 2005 study conducted by condom maker Durex

17

Number of months the average engagement lasts

26

Average age of brides in 2007

28

Average age of grooms in 2007

53

Percent of ceremonies held in a church

83

*Number of times record-holding couple
Lauren Blair and David E. Blair
had renewed their vows between
1984 and 2004*

*Percent of newlyweds that take
a honeymoon; only 35 percent of
them have valid passports*

169

Average number of guests at the wedding reception

$877

*Average cost of a wedding cake
in New York City*

1907

Year the British Parliament passed the Deceased
Wife's Sister's Marriage Act, which removed the
prohibition forbidding a man to marry the sister
of his deceased wife

7,355

Pounds of pasta in which a couple stood while being married on TV on Valentine's Day 2004

7,451

Number of couples that locked lips simultaneously in Hungary in 2007 to try and beat the previous kissing world record of 6,613

$27,000

What the average wedding in the United States now costs

166,000

Number of weddings that took place in Istanbul, Turkey, in 2006, making it the top wedding city in the world (Las Vegas came in second with 114,00.)

2.3 million

Number of couples wed in the United States annually

$874 million

Amount Soraya Khashoggi got in her divorce from Saudi businessman Adnan Khashoggi, which is the largest cast settlement in divorce history and today would equal $1.8 billion

MARK HER WORDS

An intelligent woman
who reads the marriage contract
and then goes into it deserves
all the consequences.

—Isadora Duncan

Men and women, women and men.
It will never work.

—Erica Jong

Sometimes I wonder
if men and women
really suit each other.
Perhaps they should live
next door and just visit
now and then.

—Katharine Hepburn

It is always **incomprehensible to a man** that a woman should ever **refuse an offer of marriage.**

—Jane Austen

Marriage is a fine institution— but I'm not ready for an institution.

—Mae West

Liberty is a better husband

than love to many of us.

—Louisa May Alcott

If you want to sacrifice **the admiration of many men** for the **criticism of one,** go ahead, get married.

—Katharine Houghton Hepburn,
mother of never-wed film legend Katharine Hepburn

I think a single woman's
biggest problem is coping
with the people who are
trying to marry her off!

—Helen Gurley Brown

If your **head tells you one thing** and your **heart tells you another,** before you do anything, you should first decide whether you have a **better head or a better heart.**

—Marilyn vos Savant

Any woman who accepts aloneness as the natural by-product of success is accepting the punishment for a crime she didn't commit.

—Marlo Thomas

Jealousy is not the barometer by which depth of love can be read. It merely records the degree of the lover's insecurity.

—Margaret Mead

Love is moral even without legal marriage, but marriage is immoral without love.

—Ellen Key

No man ever prospered
in the world **without**
the consent and cooperation
of his wife.

—Abigail Adams

The first time you buy a house,

you think how pretty it is and sign the check.

The second time you look to see

if the basement has termites.

It's the same with men.

—Lupe Vélez

The more I see of men the more I like dogs.

—Madame de Stael

I married the first man I ever kissed.
When I tell this to my children
they just about throw up.

—Former First Lady Barbara Bush

Marrying a man is like buying **something you've been admiring** for a long time in a shop window. You may love it when you get it home, **but it doesn't always go with everything in the house.**

—Jean Kerr

I think men who have a pierced ear are

better prepared for marriage.

They've experienced pain and bought jewelry.

—Rita Rudner

For marriage to be **a success**,
every woman and every man
should have **her and his
own bathroom.**
The end.

—Catherine Zeta-Jones

I will love, honor, cherish—
but not obey.

—Rosalie Slaughter Morton

CHAPTER 5

Food for Thought

NO MATTER HOW you slice it, food ranks high on our list of everyday pleasures. Few things deliver such instant, encapsulated happiness like a cookie still warm from the oven or a plate of ribs so smothered in barbecue sauce that you require a liberal amount of wet-naps at meal's end. It's not *that* hard to believe that if one could only buy the world a Coke, every country in the land might come together to sing in perfect harmony. Our taste buds are so easily tempted (and our diets so easily abandoned) that one has to wonder if the stomach has a mind of its own. It plays such gracious host to junk food and calorie-laden confections, yet turns a cold shoulder to the likes of brussels sprouts and bran flakes. The following pages are sure to whet the appetite of any epicurean. Our advice: Don't read them on an empty stomach.

LITTLE SLICES OF HEAVEN

Friday family night fix. Mid-meeting munchie. Diet buster. Cram session craving. Gourmet grub. Pizza is the world's most ubiquitous food, so it makes sense to deliver the deep dish on this near-spiritual sustenance.

Pizza is a $41-billion-plus per-year industry. There are approximately 69,000 pizzerias in the United States, and collectively, Americans eat approximately one hundred acres of pizza each day, which is 350 slices per second.

Pizza, as we know it, is an import from Italy, although there is evidence that many ancient Middle Eastern cultures ate unleavened bread seasoned with spices and oils and baked in mud ovens. It was a traditional nosh of Naples peasants until baker Raffaele Esposito prepared a pizza especially for the 1889 visit of King Umberto and Queen Margherita. Yes, *that* Margherita. The red tomatoes, green basil, and white mozzarella represented the colors of the homeland's flag. Good reviews from royalty helped the recipe spread across the rest of the boot country. While Neapolitans get the credit for turning a round mound into a national dish and an international phenomenon, the ingredients are actually quite multicultural. Using circular bread as an edible plate was a Greek custom. Tomatoes, originally feared to be poisonous, were introduced by Spanish sailors who found them in the New World, and true mozzarella (made from water buffalo milk) has its origins in India.

Pizza migrated to America with the Italians. The first U.S. pizzeria was established in 1905 by Gennaro Lombardi in New York City at 53⅓ Spring Street. The national fervor for the food ignited after World War II GIs returned home with a taste for the real deal that they had been eating overseas. Perhaps some had even dined at the Antica Pizzeria Port'Alba in Naples, which is widely regarded as the world's first pizzeria. Originally a snack stall catering to peddlers in 1738, it became a proper pizza joint in 1830 and still serves slices today.

October is National Pizza Month.
The celebration began in 1987.

Pepperoni is by far America's favorite topping with 251,770,000 lbs. consumed per year, yet women are twice as likely as men to order vegetarian toppings. Other countries have some very different ideas about what makes the best addition to their pies. In Japan, squid and *mayo jaga* (a mayonnaise, potato, and bacon combo) are popular, while Indians prefer pickled ginger, minced mutton, and tofu. Brazil gets healthy with green peas, whereas Russians serve a fishy concoction called *mockba* (sardines, tuna, mackerel, salmon, and onions).

Half of all pizzas are purchased on Fridays and Saturdays, but the biggest sales day is Sunday. Super Bowl Sunday, incidentally, garners the most single-day pizza sales each year. In fact, nearly fifty percent of the Pizza Hut chain's deliveries and carry-outs occur in the two hours prior to kick-off and during the first hour of the Super Bowl.

Ever wonder about what the three dots stand for in the Domino's Pizza logo? They represent the first three Domino's Pizza stores. The plan was to add a dot whenever a new store was added, but considering the current store count is seven thousand-plus strong it would be an impossible tradition to continue.

Hostess with the Mostest

Since the Hostess line began in 1925 as an offshoot of the Continental Baking Company (the folks behind Wonder Bread as well), it has been putting smiles on the faces of kids and workers lucky enough to find one of these desserts at the bottom of their lunchbox. Here are some tidbits about their trademark treats that take the cake.

The Hostess Cup Cake, one of the brand's original products and now the best-selling snack cake in history, was invented in 1919 by a mystery chef. It was baking executive D.R. "Doc" Rice who added the snack's seven signature squiggles and creamy vanilla filling in 1950. Golden Cup Cakes (made with yellow cake) debuted in 1999.

A Florida woman named Suzanne Rutland claims to have eaten more than fifty thousand Cup Cakes (as many as four a day) since childhood when she founded a Cup Cake Club. The secret password was "creamy."

Twinkies were the brainchild of Jimmy Dewar in 1930. Seeing a gap in the Depression-era marketplace for an inexpensive dessert, the Illinois bakery manager made use of the Little Shortbread Fingers shortcake pans, which were previously only used during the summer strawberry season. His treat remained nameless until he was on his way to St. Louis to present the product. He found inspiration in a billboard along the highway advertising Twinkle Toe Shoes.

Originally, Twinkies were filled with banana creme, but a ration on the yellow fruit during World War II forced the company to switch to the vanilla center that is still used today.

Hostess sells five hundred million Twinkies each year. They claim to turn out one thousand per minute. Making that massive amount of spongy goodness requires eight million pounds of sugar, seven million pounds of flour, and one million eggs. Chicago, where the factory is located, is coincidentally the American city with the highest per capita Twinkie consumption.

Despite a Maine teacher's claims that a Twinkie that he kept atop his chalkboard for thirty years was still edible, Hostess maintains that the delicacy's shelf life is realistically closer to twenty-five days. This can be attributed to the fact that the recipe calls for no dairy-based ingredients. They are made of flour, three kinds of sugar, oil, eggs, and chemicals (mainly preservatives and stabilizers).

President Clinton included a Twinkie in the White House Millennium Council's time capsule in 1999 calling it "an enduring American icon." Considering the rumored shelf life, it may still be edible when the collection is dug up.

Ho Hos, the tubular cream-filled chocolate cakes covered by a confectionary chocolate shell, date back to 1967 when a San Francisco bakery produced them by hand. In 1999, a contest to find the country's nuttiest celebrity laugh was launched to celebrate the arrival of Nutty Ho Hos (the original roll plus chopped peanuts). Voters picked Eddie Murphy's chortle as No. 1 followed by the guffaws and giggles of Phyllis Diller, Roseanne Barr, and Pee-Wee Herman.

Suzy Qs—either banana-flavored or devil's food oblong sandwich cakes filled with white creme—were not named for the dance step, the song, the recording artist, or the popular slang nickname. They actually were named after the daughter of Cliff Isaacson, who was VP of Continental Bakeries when the snacks debuted in 1961.

The round hockey-puck-style cakes now known as Ding Dongs used to have a variety of names, including King Dons and Big Wheels, depending on where in the United States you purchased them. The now standardized moniker is a tribute to the chiming bells used in Hostess' first TV commercials.

Twinkies have even appeared in court. When Minneapolis city council candidate George Belair served Twinkies and other refreshments to two senior citizens' groups in 1985, he was indicted for bribery and newspapers dubbed the ordeal "Twinkiegate." Although the charges were eventually dropped, the case led to the Minnesota Fair Campaign Act, more commonly called the "Twinkie law," which has since been repealed. The "Twinkie Defense" was another term coined by journalists. They were covering the 1979 trial of former San Francisco supervisor Dan White, who was accused of shooting Mayor George Moscone and Supervisor Harvey Milk. White's lawyers argued that he suffered from severe depression exacerbated by a junk food binge, and this defense led to his conviction on a lesser charge.

Christopher Sell is credited with inventing the fried Twinkie at the ChipShop, his restaurant in Brooklyn, New York. Now a big seller at county fairs, the cake is frozen, dipped in batter, placed onto a Popsicle stick or wood skewer, and deep-fried.

A Taste for Romance

Can one type of appetite trigger another? The following everyday foods are far from commonplace thanks to their suspected aphrodisiac qualities.

Chocolate—Aztec emperor Montezuma reputedly drank fifty cups of hot chocolate every day to enhance his romantic prowess. Not a bad idea, considering he was thought to have approximately six hundred female companions.

Asparagus—During the reign of Louis XV, notorious sexpot Madame de Pompadour considered asparagus to be a prized produce turn-on. (Its suggestive shape may have had a little something to do with it.)

Chilies—Hot and spicy peppers are believed to get the heart pounding and the blood pumping thanks to a chemical called capsaicin. Women in ancient civilizations sometimes even bathed in water that had been steeped with chilies.

Coffee—The caffeine in this popular beverage stimulates your system, allowing you to pull an all-nighter, if you get the drift.

Honey—For one month following their nuptials, medieval newlyweds drank mead, a drink made from fermented honey, which, they believed, was a conjugal elixir of sorts. The practice is thought to have inspired the term "honeymoon."

Oysters—Legendary ladies' man, Casanova, consumed fifty raw oysters each day for breakfast, or so the story goes. He may have been onto something. In 2005, researchers determined that the mollusks are rich in amino acids that trigger increased levels of sex hormones.

Avocados—The Aztecs believed that the fruit hanging from an avocado tree resembled a man's, well…need we say more?

Garlic—You might think garlic breath is a romance-killer, but the potent cooking ingredient is believed to improve blood circulation and stir up passions. For that reason, some Buddhist monks exclude garlic from their diets.

Other Aphrodisiacs—Grapes, strawberries, artichokes, ginger, black beans, rosemary, pine nuts, alcohol, figs, fennel, celery, cloves, onion, nutmeg, saffron, chick peas, peaches, truffles, and lobster.

Finally, you won't find the following list of libido enhancers at your friendly neighborhood supermarket, but they've been touted as powerful love potions, nonetheless: Fresh snake blood, dried lizard powder, shark fin, ambergris (a waxy substance found in whales), jackal or boar bile, reindeer antler, rhinoceros horn, Spanish fly (a type of beetle found in parts of southern Europe.)

COOKIE CLUTTER

Do(ugh)n't skip this page! You needn't be the Cookie Monster to appreciate these fast facts about one of the world's favorite desserts.

Americans consume more than two billion cookies a year, and they are eaten in 95.2 percent of U.S. households. And to think, they were first made by accident. Cooks once used a small amount of cake batter to test their oven temperature before baking a large cake. The testers were called *koekje*, which means "little cake" in Dutch. The earliest cookie-style cakes are thought to date back to seventh-century Persia, one of the first countries to cultivate sugar.

In 1937, legend has it that a Massachusetts innkeeper named Ruth Wakefield ran out of baker's chocolate while making cookies from a colonial recipe at The Toll House Inn and Restaurant. She improvised by dropping a broken-up bar of semisweet chocolate into the flour, butter, and brown sugar dough and changed the dessert landscape forever with what is considered the first chocolate chip cookie.

Biscotti means "twice cooked" and is the generic term for cookies in Italian. To make traditional biscotti, dough logs are baked until golden brown. The logs are then sliced and the individual pieces are baked again to achieve their characteristic dryness.

In 1912, Nabisco introduced the Oreo, basically two chocolate wafers held together with white creamy filling. During the product's first ninety years, more than four hundred fifty billion Oreos were consumed.

The ANZAC (Australian and New Zealand Army Corps) wafer is Australia's national biscuit and it even has its own holiday (April 25). Its origins can be traced back to the oatcake recipes Scottish immigrants brought to this island country in the 1800s. Because of their extremely long shelf life, they became the food of choice to send loved ones serving overseas during World War I, when mail could take two months or more to be delivered. Made with flour and water only, the biscuits can be stored without refrigeration for years.

It's alleged that Peter the Great and his wife, Catherine, so enjoyed ladyfingers, a popular French royal indulgence since the 11th century, that when visiting France's King Louis XV they bought his baker and immediately sent him home to Russia. Nowadays it is much easier to enjoy the spongy cookie. Virtually all the commercially available ladyfingers in America since 1901 are the product of Specialty Bakers, Inc., a small bakery on the banks of the Susquehanna River in Marysville, Pennsylvania.

Brownies are considered bar cookies. Their origin is uncertain, although the first published recipe for them appeared in an 1897 Sears, Roebuck catalog.

There are two possible inspirations for fortune cookies. To coordinate an uprising against Mongolian occupiers, Chinese revolutionaries slipped secret messages on rice paper into cakes filled with a lotus nut paste that was strongly disliked by Mongolians. But it's also a Chinese custom to send out cake rolls with a message inside announcing the birth of a child.

Peanut-based cookie recipes were three of the 105 suggestions found in African-American botanist/educator George Washington Carver's 1916 research paper, "How to Grow the Peanut and 105 Ways of Preparing it for Human Consumption."

The sale of cookies to finance Girl Scout troop activities started in 1917, five years after the organization began, when the Mistletoe Troop in Muskogee, Oklahoma, held a sale in the high school cafeteria. Most chapters sold items they baked personally until the national organization began the process of licensing the first commercial baker to handle their fundraising food production in 1936. During World War II, butter, sugar, and flour shortages prompted the clubs to shift to calendar sales. The three original mass-produced flavors—still available today— were sandwich, shortbread, and Thin Mints.

Some cookies are traditionally associated with specific celebrations. Pizzelles (a.k.a. sweet bread pancake cookies pressed with ornate irons) are a signature part of the menu during the Festival of the Snakes/Feast Day of San Domenico in Colcullo, Italy. Springerle are traditional Bavarian Christmas cookies that originated at Julfest, a midwinter celebration of pagan Germanic tribes. The holiday called for animal sacrifice, but poor people who couldn't afford to lose their livestock instead gave animal-shaped cookies as tokens of their devotion. This eventually morphed into white, anise-flavored stamped cookies and animal-print molds.

The snickerdoodle is the most mysterious member of the cookie family. Many food historians think they were invented in 19th century New England because they were known for naming treats silly things like "plunkets" and "cry babies." *The Joy of Cooking* attributes the cookie to Germany, suggesting the name is a corruption of the German word *schneckennudeln* (a cinnamon-dusted sweet roll), but it may also be a contraction of Saint Nicholas, and, therefore, Dutch. It's also possible that these treats are a relative of the British-inspired Christmas cakes and cookies common on the Eastern Seaboard of the United States.

NAME-DROPPING

Hershey's went the easy route in 1978 when naming their new candy bar a Whatchamacallit. These other culinary creations took the eponymous route. They're named after the people who cooked them up or inspired them.

BEEF WELLINGTON

After helping vanquish Napoleon at the Battle of Waterloo, Arthur Wellesley, 1st Duke of Wellington, went down in history as the inspiration behind this pastry-wrapped package of pate and beef. Its shape and baked sheen is thought to resemble the riding boots he wore.

GRANNY SMITH APPLE

Maria Ann Smith, a grandma from New South Whales, Australia, is said to have discovered the first of this type of tart, green fruit in her yard. She conjectured that the new variety first sprouted from the remains of a French crab apple that she had tossed out in her garden.

Salisbury Steak

Meat good. Veggies bad. That's what English physician Dr. James H. Salisbury figured when he created this future staple of TV dinners in 1888. In his day, the concoction was just plain old cooked hamburger. Believing starch and vegetables were toxic to digestive systems, he advised patients to partake of his "Salisbury Treatment" three times a day.

Chicken Tetrazzini

This creamy pasta with chicken, mushrooms, and breadcrumbs was supposedly first dished up in San Francisco in the early 1900s in honor of legendary opera soprano Luisa Tetrazzini.

Cobb Salad

In 1936, Robert H. Cobb, owner of the Brown Derby restaurant in Hollywood, was jonesing for a late-night snack. He rummaged through the fridge and, in this case, hunger was the mother of invention. He tossed together hard-boiled egg, bacon, avocado, lettuce, and blue cheese to concoct this now revered salad.

Fettucine Alfredo

Italian chef Alfredo di Lelio created the classic parmesan-flavored pasta dish in the early 1920s at his restaurant in Rome. After actors Mary

Pickford and Douglas Fairbanks sampled the rich dish on their honeymoon trip, they raved about it to friends when they returned stateside, thereby sealing its fate as a staple of Italian restaurants henceforth.

MELBA TOAST/PEACH MELBA

Australia-born opera diva Nellie Melba must have had a serious set of pipes to merit having not one, but a variety of recipes named in her honor. The dry, toasted cracker and the fruity dessert remain the most widely consumed.

CRÊPES SUZETTE

As the story goes, "Suzette" was the name of a woman dining with England's Prince Edward VII at the Monte Carlo restaurant, Café de Paris in 1895. Henri Charpentier claimed credit for inventing the sweet, brandy-flavored crepe dish here purely by accident, saying that when the prince tasted the dish, he requested that it be named after his date.

LOBSTER NEWBURG

Ben Wenburg, a frequent patron of New York's Delmonico's restaurant, first showed the proprietor how to make this rich seafood dish, which was consequently named in his honor. Legend has it the letters were transposed in retaliation after Wenburg and the restaurant's management had a falling out.

Bing Cherry

Oregon horticulturalist Seth Lewelling first cultivated this variety of fruit in the 1870s and, giving credit where credit was due, named it after his nursery's Chinese foreman, Ah Bing.

Graham Cracker

Believing whole-wheat flour was far healthier than white flour, a prudish American clergyman named Sylvester Graham advocated this nutritional cracker. He also believed that all form of pastries excluding fruit pies were "among the most pernicious articles of human ailment."

Eggs Benedict

This one's up for grabs: Some say this classic breakfast dish began as a hangover cure for one Lemuel Benedict, a New York stock broker who beseeched workers at the Waldorf Hotel to oblige his cravings for toast, poached eggs, bacon, and a side of Hollandaise sauce. Others insist Delmonico's restaurant devised the recipe after it was suggested by a Mrs. Le Grand Benedict.

BY THE NUMBERS

12

Minutes it took Takeru Kobayashi to eat 50 hot dogs at the 86th
Annual Nathan's Famous Fourth of July Hot Dog Eating Contest,
which broke a world record

20

*Percentage of reduction in the risk of heart disease
when one eats at least eight servings of fruits
and vegetables a day*

31

Number of teaspoons of sugar the average
American eats each day

56

Percentage of American adults that sip coffee daily

*An average American eats this many
restaurant meals a year, with the biggest
spenders being Seattleites*

90

Percent of households in the United States that consume
ice cream and related frozen desserts

166

Bottles of water consumed by
the average American each year

174

*Number of original ice cream flavors
that have been retired to the flavor
graveyard at Ben & Jerry's*

200

Amount of calories in one
original glazed donut from
Krispy Kreme

300

Cost, in dollars, of the Heal the Bay Martini,
which comes with a real black pearl in the glass,
at Los Angeles' Abode restaurant

1.2 to 1.4 million

Number of hens on the average-sized
modern chicken farm

1.54 billion

*Gallons of ice cream and related frozen
desserts produced in the United States in 2005*

MARK HER WORDS

I don't eat junk foods and
I don't think junk thoughts.

—Peace Pilgrim

Maybe [women] **weren't at the Last Supper,** but we're certainly **going to be at the next one.**

—Bella Abzug

Everything you see, I owe to spaghetti.

—Sophia Loren

Too many cooks may
spoil the broth,
but it only takes one
to burn it.

—Julia Child

I come from a family where

gravy is considered a beverage.

—Erma Bombeck

Most turkeys taste better **the day after;** my mother's tasted better **the day before.**

—Rita Rudner

Ask your child what he wants for dinner **only if he's buying.**

—Fran Lebowitz

Roast Beef, Medium, is not only a food. It is a philosophy. Seated at Life's Dining Table, with the menu of Morals before you, your eye wanders a bit over the entrées, the hors d'oeuvres, and the things à la, though you know that Roast Beef, Medium, is safe and sane, and sure.

—Edna Ferber

A good cook is like
a sorceress who
dispenses happiness.

—Elsa Schiaparelli

One cannot think well, love well, sleep well,

if one has not dined well.

—Virgina Woolf

Stressed spelled backwards
is **desserts.** Coincidence?
I think not!

—Anonymous

There are two kinds
of people in the world:
those who love chocolate,
and communists.

—Leslie Moak Murray

Strength is the capacity

to break a chocolate bar into four pieces

with your bare hands—and then eat

just one of the pieces.

—Judith Viorst

Ice cream

is happiness

condensed.

—Jessi Lane Adams

CHAPTER 6

That's Entertainment!

IF ALL THE WORLD'S A STAGE

and the men and women merely players, why can't the rest of us command a seven-figure, three-picture deal or line the walls of our home with solid gold records? *Talent*, you suggest? We'll give you that one except where Tara Reid and William Hung are concerned. The lifestyles of the rich and famous, especially the trainwreck ones, are endlessly fascinating, and, to that end, we've dug up the dirt on Hollywood heavy hitters, jukebox heroes, and rising stars. We'll take you on location and behind the scenes. So pop some popcorn and strike up the band. We're rolling out the red carpet for this last chapter!

CHICK FLICKS

You'll laugh! You'll cry! You'll fall in love with this insider information about films that females have flocked to.

To get into character for *The Notebook*, Ryan Gosling lived in South Carolina, rowed the Ashley River each morning, and apprenticed with a furniture maker, building the kitchen table and two Adirondack chairs seen in the tearjerker. He also changed his physical appearance. It took the actor two months to grow a beard and, after filming scenes that occur later in the timeline, he had to lose twenty pounds over Christmas break to play the young Noah. He also wore brown contacts to match the peepers of James Garner, who portrays Noah in the present-day sequences.

Rom-com scribe extraordinaire Nora Ephron set the bookstore scene in *When Harry Met Sally...* in Shakespeare & Co., a small chain of New York bookstores forced out of business when Barnes & Noble came to the neighborhood. Ephron then used that company's sob story as a model for the plot of another of her hits, *You've Got Mail.*

Dirty Dancing takes place in the Catskills but was filmed several states away. Mountain Lake Resort near Roanoke, Virginia, was used for the resort exteriors. Much of the rest of the film was shot around North Carolina's Lake Lure. Filming in North Carolina was plagued by uncooperative weather. It started with sweltering heat that caused ten people to pass out after twenty-five minutes of filming. Delays forced shooting to continue into the fall, and set decorators had to spray-paint the turning leaves green because the story takes place during the summer. Unfortunately for Jennifer Grey and Patrick Swayze, the trademark lake scene wasn't scheduled until October when temperatures dropped into the forties. The director only used wide shots whenever the actors were wet, because their lips were blue and quivering.

The magical land in *The Wonderful Wizard of Oz* was thought up when author L. Frank Baum, looked at his filing cabinet's drawer labeled O–Z.

To help achieve Captain Jack Sparrow's playfulness and jaunty demeanor, Johnny Depp is rumored to have worn an earpiece that pumped music into his ear while filming the *Pirates of the Caribbean* trilogy.

In *The Bodyguard*, Whitney Houston and Kevin Costner's characters go to the movies for date night. They see Akira Kurosawa's *Yojimbo*, which was released in the United States under the name *The Bodyguard.* Incidentally, Costner's haircut in the film was a tribute to Steve McQueen, for whom the part had originally been written.

Bert and Ernie on *Sesame Street* were named after the cop and the taxi driver in Frank Capra's *It's a Wonderful Life*.

Talk about giving 'em the cold shoulder. Julia Roberts suggested that the crew of *Sleeping with the Enemy* strip down to their skivvies so that they could empathize with her while she had to suffer through a chilly outdoor water scene.

Renée Zellweger pounded Snickers bars, pizza, donuts, and chocolate milkshakes in order to gain the twenty pounds necessary to embody diarist and yo-yo dieter, Bridget Jones.

In *The African Queen*, when Katharine Hepburn was forced to climb into murky water in the Belgian Congo, the director had the prop men fire bullets into the water to scare the crocodiles away.

Although he figured into the fantasies of legions of ladies, Clark Gable didn't impress his *Gone with the Wind* costar, Vivien Leigh, who went on record about how awful his dentures smelled. Frequent collaborator Lana Turner laughed about the time that he kissed her so forcefully in a scene that he dislodged the gum that she had stashed in her teeth during takes. When he pulled away, they were attached by a ribbon of sticky stuff. Gable didn't fair any better off screen. Joan Crawford said, "He wasn't a satisfying lover." Carole Lombard called him "the worst lay in town." Even his first girlfriend noted "his ears were too big" and he was "all feet" on the dance floor.

Nicole Kidman is accident-prone on set. She broke a rib and tore cartilage in her knee after slipping on the stairs while she was high-kicking her way down for *Moulin Rouge!* More recently, she was involved in a vehicle crash on the set of *The Invasion,* thankfully suffering only minor scrapes and bruises. More painful still were the budget woes on her latest collaboration with *Rouge* director Baz Luhrmann, a rural epic called *Australia.* When the Faraway Downs homestead set was unexpectedly flooded, production had to relocate to Sydney until it dried out.

When Kate Bosworth auditioned for Robert Redford's *The Horse Whisperer*, the aspiring thespian brought a family Christmas card as her headshot. We're guessing it was her previous experience as an equestrian champion that helped her seal the deal. She wasn't quite as lucky when it came time to film the girl surfer drama *Blue Crush* as she had never stepped onto a board in her life. To tackle that role, she put on twenty pounds of muscle and took surfing lessons. Riding waves became a regular hobby post-premiere.

Penelope Cruz looked bootilicious in her Oscar-nominated turn in *Volver*, and she owes partial credit to a prosthetic padded behind. She managed to fill out those cleavage-baring tops all on her own, however.

Making *The Accidental Tourist* was a family affair: Director Lawrence Kasdan cast his son, Jacob, as Scott Canfield and his wife, Meg, as a receptionist while his other son, Jon, appears in the doctor's office scene. Meg also plays a nurse in Kasdan's *Body Heat.*

Michelle Pfeiffer regrets not keeping one of her sexy leather catsuits from her stint as *Batman*'s feline-esque foe. At the time, she couldn't stand the thought of another day in the costume, so she only kept her prop whip. She learned her lesson and put in her requests for some of her *Hairspray* dresses while still in production. Speaking of the 2007 version of *Hairspray*, the original film's writer/director, John Waters, cameos as a flasher during the first musical number, and the original Tracy Turnblad, Ricki Lake, plays a talent scout in the film's big finish.

STAR SEARCH

Thousands of people move to Hollywood, New York, and Nashville every year hoping to get discovered. Usually it happens after paying their dues in classes, auditions, cattle calls, contests, local theater, and open-mic nights. But for the following folks, their showbiz dreams found them when they least expected it.

A camera crew roaming the stands at a 1989 British Columbia Lions football game helped Pamela Anderson go from fan to famous. When the future Baywatcher, wearing a Labatt's Beer T-shirt, appeared on the Jumbotron, the crowd went wild and she was brought down to the fifty-yard line to be interviewed. Brewery executives immediately hired her as a spokesperson and the popular "Blue Zone Girl" campaign led to other commercial work and the interest of Hugh Hefner. She has since graced the cover of *Playboy* more than any other woman in the magazine's history.

Wonder if *The OC* alum Mischa Barton was wearing Keds (a footwear brand she now touts) when she delivered a self-penned monologue about turtles when she was eight? A talent scout who was there with his children caught the riveting performance and talked to Barton's parents. A year later she was treading the boards for Pulitzer Prize-winning playwright Tony Kushner.

Actress Shannyn Sossamon spun records at Gwyneth Paltrow's birthday party, which in turn spun into a Hollywood career. She was spotted in the deejay booth by a casting director who introduced her to director Brian Helgeland. The filmmaker was looking for a fresh face to play princess opposite hunky Heath Ledger in *A Knight's Tale*, and he instantly pegged Sossamon to be the flick's leading lady.

A party proved prosperous for Cameron Diaz, who caught the eye of a fellow guest, photographer Jeff Dunas. He snapped a few shots of the then-sixteen-year-old blonde, which led her to a modeling contract with Elite within days of the shindig. Prince's people, meanwhile, snapped up sexpot Carmen Electra after seeing her dancing at a club called Spice. Mariah Carey was working as a coat-checker/waitress when she met music mogul and future husband Tommy Mottola at a Manhattan fete. Who says it doesn't pay to party?

A retired MGM contract player, Norma Shearer knew real talent when she saw it…in a photograph on the desk of a ski resort employee. Struck by the lovely face framed on a proud pop's desk, Shearer borrowed the picture and showed it to bigwigs at her old studio. They, too, saw potential and brought in the then-college student (studying psychology and music) for a screen test. Soon that girl, Janet Leigh, was bathing in offers including one that required her to step into the shower at the Bates Motel with acclaimed auteur Alfred Hitchcock.

Avril Lavigne garnered her first manager after he saw her singing in a local bookstore in Canada while she was still a teenager.

Simply going about their daily business is all some wannabes have to do to get noticed. Sweater Girl Lana Turner was discovered at Schwab's Drugstore lunch counter. Charisma Carpenter (*Buffy the Vampire Slayer*) and supermodel Carol Alt were waiting tables when approached by agents. On the hunt for a young blonde to play a bloodsucker in *Interview with a Vampire*, a casting director happened upon a ten-year-old LeeLee Sobieski eating in her school cafeteria. She didn't book that part. (It went to Kirsten Dunst.) But the agent kept her info and scored her another role soon after. Eating also led to a future in film for Natalie Portman, who was spotted by a Revlon scout at a pizza parlor in 1991.

Kate Moss went from one kind of runway to another when a modeling scout spied the fourteen-year-old waif waiting out a layover at New York's JFK airport on her way home from a holiday in the Bahamas.

Hanging out at the mall and going to the movies can be resumé-building experiences. That's exactly how Jorja Fox (CSI), Ashley Tisdale (*High School Musical*), Victoria's Secret cover girl Adriana Lima, and Tricia Helfer (the new *Battlestar Galactica*) all found fame.

Talk about special delivery. While dropping off a package at an Orlando studio, a FedEx worker overheard fourteen-year-old Mandy Moore singing her heart out. The delivery man offered to pass along her unfinished demo to his friend at Epic Records. The favor landed Moore a record deal by the time she was a freshman in high school.

MUSIC MINUTAE

Listen up! We've collected a ton of trivia on the singers and performers who rock your world.

Growing up, Gwen Stefani was a huge fan of the 1965 movie musical *The Sound of Music* and its star Julie Andrews. The upbeat tune "I Have Confidence" inspired the first single off Stefani's sophomore album, *The Sweet Escape*, and she later sampled "The Lonely Goatherd" in her single, "Wind It Up."

President George W. Bush gave Kenny Chesney boots made for rockin' when the country cutie agreed to perform at a White House dinner for Australian Prime Minister John Howard. The custom kickers were made by Rocky Carroll of Houston's RJ's Boot Co. and featured black eel skin inlays, the singer's initials, and the flags of the United States and Australia. The priceless pair goes great with the skinny singer's twenty-nine-inch waist.

Paul McCartney and his ex, Heather Mills, used the same divorce attorneys that duked it out for Prince Charles and Princess Diana.

J. Lo isn't the only nickname singer/actress/designer/dancer/producer Jennifer Lopez answers to: Her childhood friends from the block nicknamed her "The Supernova" because of her unflappable ambition and talent, and her first husband, Ojani Noa, called her "*La Guitarra*" because he thought her body was shaped like a guitar.

Many of today's most popular musicians got their start in TV. Fergie from the Black Eyed Peas provided the voice of Sally Brown in several *Peanuts* cartoon specials before joining the cast of *Kids Incorporated* alongside future stars Jennifer Love Hewitt and Mario Lopez. The Pussycat Dolls lead singer Nicole Scherzinger hit high notes on the reality show *Popstars* as a member of the constructed group Eden's Crush. Christina Aguilera, Britney Spears, and 'N Sync's JC Chasez and Justin Timberlake all donned mouse ears on *The Mickey Mouse Club*.

Speaking of JT, the Tennessee-reared Grammy winner prizes his grandmother's cooking over any five-star dinner spot, which is why she sends him regular care packages of blueberry jam, squash relish, and pecan pie when he is on tour. Fans can get a taste of her delicacies by making a reservation at the singer's New York eatery, Southern Hospitality, where many items are made using her original recipes.

Kelly Clarkson's family pooled their money and bought her a keyboard for Christmas when she was in the fourth grade. It was on that Casio that she wrote her first song.

Even Bono needs a little help from his friends from time to time. While he has written almost all of the lyrics throughout U2's multi-decade career, the words to "The Ground Beneath Her Feet" were actually taken from author Salman Rushdie's book of the same name. When he finished the novel, the author sent it to the pop star for his opinion, and the prose inspired a melody.

Forever the businesswoman, a young Beyoncé Knowles used to charge houseguests five dollars each to watch her perform in the living room. By anyone's standards, this was a bargain as tickets to her recent shows would set you back at least seventy dollars.

Fall Out Boy made headlines when they announced that their hemoglobin was going to be used in a run of limited-edition posters made by bassist Pete Wentz' brother. They weren't the first stars to give sanguine samples. In 1977, comic publisher Marvel mixed Kiss members' fluids in with the red ink that colored the first Kiss comic. Perennially troubled performer Pete Doherty has done a series of paintings using blood as a medium that routinely fetch one thousand pounds. That's what we call O positive publicity.

American Idol judge and ex-chart topper Paula Abdul dropped out of college when she was chosen to be a Laker Girl out of a field of seven hundred applicants. She became the head cheerleader in a record three weeks.

Crooner Michael Bublé, who spent his early years working as a commercial fisherman and singing telegram messenger, recruited his girlfriend, Emily Blunt (*The Devil Wears Prada*) to sing steamy sounds on a cover of "Me and Mrs. Jones" for his album *Irresponsible*.

The band now known as Radiohead formed when its members were students at Oxford University in the late '80s. The group was initially named On a Friday.

Rapper Bow Wow's favorite meal while recording his albums isn't Kibbles 'n Bits— it's Hawaiian Punch and turkey burgers with ketchup.

TALES FROM
TV LAND

The small screen also has its fair share of behind-the-scenes fodder. Here's some tube-worthy trivia to delight die-hard couch potatoes.

Think TV producers don't care about fan opinion? The powers-that-be on *The Closer* received so much hate mail about leading lady Kyra Sedgwick's bright red lipstick that they banished the color from future episodes. They even created a storyline about a murderous cosmetic surgeon to make the transition seem natural.

Before *Ugly Betty*'s masked lady was revealed to be a post-sex change Alex Meade, she was played by Elizabeth Penn Payne. Payne was replaced by Rebecca Romijn when the bandages came off. On the same show, producer Salma Hayek pulls triple duty—she produces, plays a ruthless magazine editor, and cameos in the *Vidas de Fuego* telenovela Betty's dad watches on TV.

Hugh Laurie's *House* character was modeled after Sherlock Holmes. The similarities don't end with the fact that both solve mysteries. House's apartment is No. 221 Apt. B, and the fictional Holmes lived at 221B Baker Street. Both characters are brilliant and cocky, love music, and suffer from a drug addiction. The good doctor's right-hand man is named Wilson, which isn't all that far off from the detective's pal, Watson.

As Peter Petrelli on NBC's superhero hit *Heroes*, Milo Ventimiglia was stoked to score the role—except for his Season One swoopy bangs. Because the character swatted at those bangs so often, fans devised drinking games to mark every instance when it happened. The actor even suggested a brain-surgery storyline so that he could shave his head, but the writers didn't go for it.

On *Grey's Anatomy*, Patrick Dempsey's McDreamy character loves ferryboats, but the show's costumers could only find him scrub caps featuring pictures of the Titanic. Maybe audiences should have considered it foreshadowing of the episode where a ferry crash almost leads to his love Meredith's drowning in a chilly sea.

While it's now hard to separate Erik Estrada from his beige *CHiPs* uniform, he almost didn't get to "protect and serve" because he had been so frequently typecast as a bad guy— like the time when he shot a priest on *Hawaii Five-O*. But once the show's creator saw how well the boots and bike fit him, the character morphed from the Italian American Poncherelli into Poncherello, network TV's first Hispanic cop.

Costumers on *Melrose Place* were instructed to make Amanda's skirts as short as possible without being lewd in order to make portrayer Heather Locklear's self-admitted "stick legs" look decent. Despite the fact that Amanda married Jack Wagner's Peter Burns in the final episode (and Locklear started dating him in real life in 2007), her favorite sex scene, and there were many to choose from, was the one that involved Grant Show's character and a desk.

The billionaire clan of Brandon Davis, party boy and ex-paramour of Mischa Barton, Paris Hilton, and Lindsay Lohan, was the inspiration for the '80s nighttime soap, *Dynasty*.

Katie Holmes recorded her *Dawson's Creek* audition tape at home in Ohio in the sewing room with her mom playing the part of Dawson. The show's creator, Kevin Williamson, thought he had found his Joey but needed Holmes to do an official screen test in LA. The trip coincided with the high school musical, so she declined, not wanting to leave her classmates up a different kind of creek. Luckily, Williamson was so sure Holmes was his girl next door that he agreed to reschedule, and she scored the part of Joey Potter, the only character to appear in all 128 episodes.

Kathryn Morris, who plays badass Det. Lilly Rush on *Cold Case*, toured with her family as a gospel group when she was a child.

On the Wisteria Lane set of *Desperate Housewives,* the grass is always greener because most of it is fake. All of the titular wisteria is plastic and silk to ensure constant big blooms. The neighborhood can be found on the Universal Studios Hollywood lot, and it's not the first time it's been used in productions, although many of the facades were remodeled for the series. The same street can be seen in *The Munsters, The New Lassie, Leave It to Beaver, Buffy the Vampire Slayer, The Burbs, Providence,* and *Gremlins.*

Scott Speedman nicknamed his former *Felicity* costar and ex-girlfriend, Keri Russell, "Homework Reminder," because she was a nerd and a goodie-goodie who always rushed them back from lunch break so as not to be tardy.

ARE THEY KID-DING?

Diesel isn't just a brand of jeans or a type of fuel anymore.
It's some singer's idea of a suitable moniker for her moppet.
Because she isn't the only star saddling her small fry with
a strange name, we compiled a chart of the more unusual
examples and the popular parent they belong to.

Celebrity	Baby Name
Courteney Cox and David Arquette	daughter: Coco (combined first two letters of mom's name)
Erykah Badu	daughter: Puma; son: Seven
Victoria "Posh Spice" and David Beckham	sons: Brooklyn, Romeo, and Cruz
Toni Braxton	sons: Denim and Diezel

Jonathan Davis (Korn vocalist)	sons: Pirate Houseman and Zeppelin
Téa Leoni and David Duchovny	son: Kyd
Will Ferrell	sons: Magnus and Mattias
Bob Geldof (Musician)	daughters: Peaches Honeyblossom, Fifi Trixibelle, Pixie, and Tiger Lily
Ginuwine (R&B crooner)	daughters: Story and Dream
Rachel Griffiths	son: Banjo
Jermaine Jackson	son: Jermajesty
Michael Jackson	son: Prince Michael, Jr. and Prince Michael II (whose nickname is Blanket); daughter Paris Michael
Anthony Kiedis (Red Hot Chili Pepper vocalist)	son: Everly Bear

Simon Le Bon (Duran Duran vocalist)	daughters: Saffron Sahara, Amber Rose, and Tallulah Pine
Jason Lee	son: Pilot Inspektor
Rapper Lil' Mo	daughters: Heaven and God'iss Love Stone
Debbon Ayer and Rob Morrow	daughter: Tu (as in Tu Morrow)
Jamie Oliver (*The Naked Chef*)	daughters: Poppy Honey and Daisy Boo
Gwyneth Paltrow	daughter: Apple
Robin Wright and Sean Penn	son: Hopper Jack
Ving Rhames	daughter: Reign Beau; son: Freedom
Anna Ryder Richardson (Designer)	daughters: Dixie Dot and Bibi Bell

Robert Rodriguez (Director)	sons: Rebel, Racer, Rocket, and Rogue; daughter: Rhiannon
Slash (Guns N' Roses guitarist)	sons: London and Cash
Kevin Smith (Director)	daughter: Harley Quinn
Shannyn Sossamon	son: Audio Science
Forest Whitaker	daughters: True, Sonnet, and Autumn; son: Ocean
Gretchen Mol and Tod Williams (director)	son: Ptolemy
Demi Moore and Bruce Willis	daughters: Rumer, Scout, and Tallulah Belle

CRUSH COURSE

Here's a hunky hodgepodge about the leading men that make ladies melt.

John Travolta isn't the only "wild hog" in Kelly Preston's life. In 1988, her then-boyfriend, George Clooney, bought her a black potbellied piglet. But when they broke up the following year, he got custody of the pet. Max was the envy of many women as he was allowed to sleep in the bed next to the salt-n-pepper stud until the porker died in 2006.

At age eleven, Denzel Washington earned eleven dollars a day at his first job sweeping floors at a barbershop. The Oscar winner's paycheck has grown substantially over the years. He earned twenty million dollars for his thirtieth movie, *Out of Time*.

Toyota Altis ads featuring Brad Pitt, the first man to be named *People*'s "Sexiest Man Alive" twice, were banned in Malaysia after the country's deputy information minister ruled that Pitt's handsome appearance could potentially make Malaysian men feel inferior.

Hugh Jackman's first job was as a gas station

attendant on the midnight-to-dawn shift.

If acting hadn't worked out for him,

he has said he would have pursued a career

as a daytime television host or a stockbroker,

despite the fact that he was a journalism

major at Sydney's University of Technology.

Be forwarned, ladies! Although his life philosophy is to sweat everyday (and those days often include bike rides with Lance Armstrong), Matthew McConaughey claims that he hasn't worn deodorant in twenty years.

Orlando Bloom, a practicing Buddhist named after 17th century British composer Orlando Gibbons, has two tattoos: a sun on his navel and the Elvish word for "nine" on his right arm (the other eight members of the fellowship from the *Lord of the Rings* films got matching ink). Bloom brought home a living souvenir from Morocco where he filmed *Kingdom of Heaven*—a black dog named Sidi.

Race car enthusiast Paul Newman, who lent his voice to the animated movie *Cars*, gave family friend Jake Gyllenhaal driving lessons on a racetrack when the *Brokeback Mountain* star was just a teenager.

As a senior at New Castle Baptist Academy high school, Ryan Phillippe was voted "Best Smile." His best friends and producing partners Breckin Meyer (*Garfield*) and Seth Green (*Buffy the Vampire Slayer*) later nicknamed him "The Boy" as in "pretty boy," because of the rabid female reactions that he encounters everywhere he goes. But he is not just a pretty face. He is a tae kwon do black belt who potty-trained his daughter single-handedly.

He may be an Oscar and Golden Globe nominee now, but when he was five, Leonardo DiCaprio was fired from his first acting gig on the children's show *Romper Room* for being disruptive. We wonder if he did one of his infamous Charles Manson impersonations, which he reportedly used to scare his junior high teachers.

Will Smith knows how to spoil his wife, Jada Pinkett Smith, on her birthday. He once made a DVD telling his wife that new clothes waited upstairs and that a car would be there in twenty minutes. She was taken to the airport and flown to San Francisco, where hubby was waiting at a restaurant she had been reading about. He also hired her favorite rap act from childhood to perform at her surprise party.

Patrick Dempsey, who collects cars and races them as a hobby, is secure enough in his manhood to let his wife, who owns the Delux Beauty cosmetics line, test new products like nail polish on him.

Although his name is featured in a popular title by the Beatles, and although he sports a tattoo of the Fab Four's lyrics, Jude Law was not named after the song, "Hey Jude." His parents took their inspiration from Thomas Hardy's tragic novel, *Jude the Obscure.*

Long after becoming a household name, Zac Efron (*Hairspray/High School Musical*) continued to drive his grandpa's dented Oldsmobile, which he nick-named Oldie. He eventually celebrated *HSM2*'s record-setting TV debut by obtaining a new Audi. He also collects baseballs signed by pros.

As a teen, Boston native Matt Damon used to break-dance for money in Harvard Square. He would later attend the university as an English literature major, but dropped out twelve credits shy of graduating to pursue acting.

BY THE NUMBERS

Number of working cattle ranches run by
Wings/Sideways star Thomas Haden
Church in his native Texas

8

*Number of married couples who share a star on
Hollywood's Walk of Fame, including Jerry Stiller
and Anne Meara, Ozzie and Harriet Nelson, Sonny
and Cher, and Les Paul and Mary Ford*

13.5

Height, in inches, of
an Oscar statue

$30

Amount the lowest-grossing movie of all time,
Zyzzyx Road, starring Tom Sizemore and
Katherine Heigl, made at the box office in 2006

40

Lucille Ball's age when
I Love Lucy debuted

82 *Number of minutes Nicole Richie spent
in jail stemming from her DUI arrest*

85

Number of costume changes
Madonna has in *Evita*, currently
a *Guinness* world record

3,000

The acreage of Michael Jackson's Santa Barbara-area Neverland Ranch, which includes an amusement park

$165,000

Amount paid by an anonymous fan for Judy Garland's ruby slippers at a 1988 auction

326,000

Number of albums 14-year-old Miley Cyrus sold in one week of her double-disc, *Hannah Montana 2/Meet Miley Cyrus*, which made her the youngest artist to have two No. 1 albums in less than a year

$600,000

The sum Mariah Carey coughed up to purchase
Marilyn Monroe's childhood piano

8.3 million

Number of hardcover editions of *Harry Potter
and the Deathly Hallows* sold in the United
States in the first 24 hours after publication
(That's an average of 5,000 a minute!)

$112 million

*What golfer Tiger Woods earns from
endorsements per year*

$350 million

The reported total worth
of the Nicole Kidman-
Tom Cruise estate when
they divorced in 2001

If you don't have **good stories** to tell on your deathbed, **what good was living?**

—Jennifer Tilly

Theatre is life. Cinema is art.

Television is furniture.

—Anonymous

Today, watching television often means fighting, violence, and foul language—and that's just deciding who gets to hold the remote control.

—Donna Gephart

Sex on television
can't hurt you
unless you fall off.

—Anonymous

Television has proved that

people will look at anything

rather than each other.

—Ann Landers

Initially, I wanted to be an ice skater, but then when I was thirteen I saw *Bye Bye Birdie*, and that was it—**I wanted to be on Broadway.**

—Liza Minnelli

Most convicted felons are just people who were not taken to museums or Broadway musicals as children.

—Libby Gelman-Waxner

After my screen test, **the director clapped his hands** gleefully and yelled, "She can't talk! She can't act! **She's sensational!"**

—Ava Gardner

If a man wants to get it right, he's looked up to and respected. If a woman wants to get it right, she's difficult and impossible. If he acts, produces, and directs, he's called multi-talented. If she does the same thing, she's called vain and egotistical.

—Barbra Streisand

Music melts all the
separate parts of our
bodies together.

—Anaïs Nin

Boredom
is a great motivator.

—Uma Thurman

In Hollywood, gratitude is public enemy No. 1.

—Hedda Hopper

Film as dream,
film as music. No art passes
our conscience in the way film
does, and **goes directly
to our feelings,** deep
down into the dark rooms
of our souls.

—Ingrid Bergman

The Last Drop

Congratulations! You made it to the end without throwing in the towel.

Unfortunately, this means it is time to rise from your relaxing soak and rejoin the world of overdue bills, unfinished term papers, nagging bosses, hungry husbands, crying babies, giant laundry piles, lazy boyfriends, those last ten stubborn pounds, late thank you cards, and sibling rivalry. No, the fizzy bath bomb didn't dissolve all your problems, just as this book didn't provide an acceptable reason to cancel on what you already know will be another terrible blind date.

Fortunately, there is a silver lining to the now deflated cloud of aromatherapy bubbles. You are leaving this sudsy sanctuary flush with new knowledge, and as the hunky plastic American hero, G.I. Joe, was fond of saying, "Knowing is half the battle."

To be fair, we realize that you didn't just finish *War & Peace*, Al Gore's report on global warming, or even the purportedly life-changing

The Secret, but you can take this newly acquired information back into your daily life and use it to your advantage. Steal a glamorous idea from Posh and Beck's big day for your own wedding planning. Impress a new client with a Louisa May Alcott quote or a statistic about how long the effects of BOTOX are noticeable. When you have to attend yet another cocktail party, never be at a loss for conversation starters. Regale guests with stories of cross-dressing popes and behind-the-scenes banter about the biggest stars. Whip up a tasty meal for the cute guy next door using chapter five's *special* ingredients to ensure what kind of dessert will be on the menu. Heck, it might even be time to finally fill out that *Jeopardy* application.

Now get out of that tub, already. We're guessing that you passed raisin state about a half hour ago.

About the Authors

Carrie Bell, a former staff writer at *Us Weekly* and *Billboard*, now strings words together as a freelance journalist for various publications including *Entertainment Weekly, People, TV Guide,* and *WWD.* This is her first book. She lives with her husband, Jeremy, and her cats, Princess Stinkeye and El Chunkquistador, in the part of Los Angeles made famous by the Pauly Shore/Brendan Fraser caveman comedy. She is on a never-ending quest for the perfect cupcake and likes her baths long, hot, and bubble-filled.

Amy Helmes is a Los Angeles-based entertainment journalist who has written several previous books for Cider Mill Press, including *Boyfriend Wisdom, Superman's Girlfriend Lois Lane in Lois Lane's Guide to Life,* and *The Wisdom of Nancy Drew.* An avid trivia buff and former *Jeopardy* contestant, the only tub time that she dislikes is the time spent cleaning it.

About Cider Mill Press
Book Publishers

Good ideas ripen with time. From seed to harvest, Cider Mill Press strives to bring fine reading, information, and entertainment together between the covers of its creatively crafted books. Our Cider Mill bears fruit twice a year, publishing a new crop of titles each spring and fall.

*Where Good Books are
Ready for Press*

Visit us on the Web at
www.cidermillpress.com
or write to us at
12 Port Farm Road
Kennebunkport, Maine 04046